Believe

A Collection of Faith, Hope, and Love

Written By
Dawn Airhart Witte and Friends

Copyright © 2022 by Dawn Airhart Witte

All rights reserved. No part of this publication may be reproduced, distributed, or transmitted in any form or by any means, including photocopying, recording, or other electronic or mechanical methods, without the prior written permission of the publisher, except in the case of brief quotations embodied in critical reviews and certain other noncommercial uses permitted by copyright law.

ISBN: 978-1-915147-83-7 (Paperback)
ISBN: 978-1-915147-84-4 (Ebook)

Book Design by HMDpublishing

"And now these three remain: faith, hope, and love. But the greatest of these is love"

Corinthians 13:13

Dedication

This book is dedicated to ALL of my children around the world. You have given me purpose and showered me with tremendous love. You are my WHY. I am grateful that you exist in this world and in my life. Keep shining your beautiful lights, because together, we can BE the change we wish to see.

Contents

Introduction 6

1. Ubuntu, I am Because we Are 10
2. Patrick Meniboon... Doubt to Impact:
   Self-Belief is Overrated 17
3. Laura Brennan Ballet... The Empowerment of Believing 25
4. Louise Bieshke... Kentucky to California 2003 32
5. Bulasio Bulumo... The Story of Buluma Bulasio 38
6. Father Jean d'Amor... God's Love
   and Forgiveness Have No Limits 43
7. Natashah Khan... How I Came to Believe 48
8. Bobby Manard... A Rose Between Two Thorns 54
9. Kunle Pelemo... Believe and Just Do It 59
10. Gail Flowers...Yellow Butterfly 65
11. Debra Hult... Not Funny, Not Fair...
    Where Was God in All of This? 68
12. Rachel Dubin... Finding Grace Through Pain... 73
13. Portia Booker... A Leak In This Old Building 79
14. Nana Kontor Nketiah... An Account of my Faith in God 85
15. Larita Rice Barnes... Prospering In a Pandemic 91
16. Luz Sanchez... Do Your Best, The Rest Leave to God 97
17. Doneza Inez Smith... I Believe in You 103
18. Valerie C. Thompson... Believe- The Word 110

Conclusion 117

Introduction

When I wrote my first book, *Be...*, in 2017, I thought about writing three books: *Be...*, *Two Be...*, and *Believe...* I did not know what *Believe...* would exactly BE (pun intended), but that title came to me, and here it is. To date, *Believe...* is the ninth book I have written, and I have also contributed to three other book collaborations. I may have imagined writing three books, but the Universe had bigger and better plans for me. When we follow our dreams, listen to the inner calling of our soul, and trust in a power that is greater than ourselves, life will expand in ways we could not even imagine. Everything happens in Divine time and Divine order, and when we have that faith—when we BELIEVE—we will see miracles, receive answers, and live fulfilling and purpose-filled lives beyond our wildest dreams.

I am so grateful to all of the authors who have contributed to this collection of faith, hope, and love. I am very blessed to have each of them in my life. They encourage and inspire me. Their stories of overcoming and believing uplift and strengthen my own beliefs. I have faith you will feel the same after reading their powerful contributions.

I am also tremendously grateful to have my daughter, Taylor Witte, contributing her amazing talents to the editing and production of this book. It has always been a dream of mine to have my daughters work with me in my mission to BE the change we wish to see. I am so honored to be their mom.

My mother was born Hindu and raised Catholic, and my father took us to a Foursquare Gospel Christian church when I was a child, but he questioned his faith and was not a firm believer in a higher power. God and faith were not something we talked about in my family. Over my lifetime, I, too, questioned my faith. I only believed in God because I was told there was a God, but I can vividly remember questioning how an all-powerful and omnipotent God could allow all the suffering that existed in the world to happen. I was just a little girl, but it made me cry to know that people and animals were hungry. If I had the power to end suffering, hunger, and poverty I would. I did not understand how God could allow these things to be. I never closed the door of belief fully, but I spent many years not knowing exactly what I believed. I have always believed, and still do, that love and kindness are why we are here. I lived my life being the type of person I wished I had in my life, but there was still that questioning within my heart and soul. I had to find my own path to my faith. And I did.

There has always been so much debate and argument about whose faith is the correct faith. People have told me that if I did not believe what they believed, or if I did not read from the book that they read, or if I did not worship God in the way they did, then I was wrong. These beliefs further pushed me away from God because I saw so much division when it came to religion.

After my daughters were adults and out on their own, I started questioning what my purpose was and why I even existed. I started on a journey of self-discovery that changed my life and cemented my faith. We will all have challenges, difficulties, and loss throughout our lifetimes. It is in those moments that we learn our greatest lessons. Some of the experiences that I have had have no explanation other than something greater than what we can see or understand in this physical world.

What I have come to believe is that faith is a personal journey between us and our higher power. I look to the universal truths that exist within all belief systems. Those truths span across Shamanism, Christianity, Judaism, Hinduism, Taoism, Buddhism, Islam, and more. Our belief in God should be something that connects and unites us. Our faith should make us happier, stronger, and better people. Our faith should make us understand the purposes and meanings of our lives.

My greatest hope for this book is to share these stories of faith and belief to help you come to your own understanding of God. When we look at the miracles and magic that surround us in every moment of our lives, we can see that we have much to be grateful for. There is a Divine power that guides us, loves us, and protects us—every one of us. If we lean into believing that our souls are eternal and that our purpose here on this earth is to do

God's work, then we will see signs and messages everyday and in all things.

I want this book to bring you hope and to inspire you to live to your highest purpose. One thing I have learned in my search for understanding is that God does not allow "bad" things to happen, *we* allow them to happen when we do not step into the calling he has for our lives. Everything and everyone is connected on this beautiful earth, and we have more power than we know when we understand this. We can BE the change we wish to see, and that is how God works. There can be miracles when we BELIEVE.

Dawn Airhart Witte

"All I have seen teaches me to trust the Creator for all I have not seen."

Ralph Waldo Emerson

Chapter 1
Ubuntu – "I am because we are."

When I started asking myself questions about why I existed and what my purpose was here on this earth, I took an amazing journey of self-discovery that changed the way I see the world and my place in it.

I had the opportunity to work with the phenomenal Laura J. Swan. She is my mentor, friend, and a truly amazing soul. I am so very blessed to know her, and I am so grateful that she came into my life exactly when she did. Laura taught me so much, and working with her literally changed my life. I was getting ready to embark on my first trip to Africa, because it was something that I had always wanted to do ever since I was a young child. I did not know why I had always felt this calling, but I had. During one of our sessions, a few weeks before I left for my trip, Laura guided me through a meditation and asked what I envisioned for my trip. I am not a great meditator, but Laura was always able to get me to a place where I could tap into the visions of my soul.

Laura asked me questions about what I wanted to see and do while I was in Africa. Truthfully, I wanted to go and meet the children I had seen in my dreams: the ones who were orphaned and were struggling for food and basic necessities; the ones who did not have a parent to love them. I love being a mom, and I feel that I have so much love to give to every child. I wanted to go there to let these children know they were loved—that I loved them even though I had never met them. I loved them because they existed. That is what I did know. As Laura guided me through the meditation, I envisioned a picture of beautiful African children wearing school uniforms. In my mind, I thought, "Well of course that picture came to you, because that is who you are going there for."

As she continued guiding me, the next image that came to me was that of a brown wall on a dirt road. The skeptic in me was thinking, "You have seen pictures like this before, so of course these are the images that you are seeing." The inner skeptic in me was very powerful. The next image that came to me was a grayish-brown wall with a PVC pipe that was cut flush with the wall. Now that vision stumped me, because I had no idea where that came from. Laura said, "Maybe you are going to bring water to them." I wasn't thinking about bringing water to anyone at that time. I was going to meet and love the children that I had dreamed about my whole life.

A few weeks later, I left for Africa on a trip that would change my life forever. Once I arrived, I was on a hunt to find that wall and that PVC pipe, because I wanted to see if that vision held some message for me. I was dubious but curious.

When I arrived at the combined school and orphanage in Ghana at which I had signed up to volunteer, I felt such peace and happiness. Everyone was so warm and welcoming, and it felt so very right in my soul. I loved being there. As volunteers, we had daily assignments, and we would wake up early in the morning to help the children bathe and get ready for school. After the children started school, we would help serve breakfast to over 800 children from gigantic, black, steaming kettles and deliver the meals to each classroom. It was hot, it was humid, and it was hard, but I loved it. After breakfast, the volunteers had a break to do whatever we wanted to do before it was time to help serve and deliver lunches. I would take that time to go to the preschool room, where there were children ranging in age from babies to five-year-olds. I absolutely loved visiting them; they were so precious, and they were happy to have someone there that absolutely loved and adored them. I will always love and adore them.

On the second day visiting the classroom, with children surrounding me and crawling all over me, I looked up to see a window in the classroom. Out of that window, I saw that same grayish-brown wall with a PVC pipe, cut flush, that I had in my vision. Chills ran throughout my body. Here, in the physical world, was something I had only seen in the vision of my mind just a few weeks before. That will be one of those moments that is etched into my memory for the rest of my days. I took a picture of it, because I never wanted to forget seeing that image. Seeing that image was one of those "aha" moments that helped cement my faith in something that cannot be explained or understood without a belief in something greater than ourselves. It was a confirmation.

Because I saw in the physical world something that I had only envisioned in my mind, I know that there is a power and a force that has a plan for my life. The seeds were planted in my heart from the time I was a little girl, but I had no idea why until I started stepping into that calling. Now I understand why it is so important to follow the callings of our hearts. We may not understand the calling when the seed is planted, but just like a plant, it takes time to grow and blossom.

Fast forward to today, I have spent nearly four months in Africa, traveling to five different countries and meeting thousands of children. My life has been transformed because I said "yes" to a dream I had held in my heart for nearly my entire life. I do not know why I felt so called to go to Africa, but I know it is part of my soul's journey. I felt a calling in my soul to go to each of the countries I have traveled to—I trusted that calling and went. I had no guarantee that things would turn out the way that they did. I did not know what to expect, but I let go of expectations and just followed my soul. My life today is greater and more beautiful because I took those leaps of faith.

After I finished my life coaching certification, I embarked on my second trip to Africa. This time, going to Ghana was not enough. I added Uganda, Kenya, and Rwanda to my itinerary. While we were driving through the villages, I saw so much poverty and lack. It broke my heart, just as it had when I was a young girl, but now I was in the midst of it rather than just imagining it. I had just been taught that we live in an abundant universe, and that if we ask God for help, he will provide. I was trying to reconcile that notion with what I was seeing in the lives of the people by which I was surrounded. I knew that those mothers were praying to God to help them feed their children. Why wasn't he answering those prayers? I could not make it make sense until it came to me: maybe I was an answer to that mother's prayer. Maybe somehow, God let me hear her prayer, and that is why I felt called to do the work I do. Why have I always felt called? Again, it hit me: we are here to do God's work here on this earth. We are all here to answer someone's prayers, and someone else is here to be an answer to ours. There are angels that walk amongst us, and I want to be one of those angels. We all have that choice.

We did indeed drill a borehole at the Savior Children's Foundation to bring clean water to the children who live and go to school where I volunteered. In addition to that borehole, we have also drilled two other boreholes in Ghana, bringing water to communities that needed it. We have built a medical bay in a community that had no medical facilities near them. We have moved our children in Sierra Leone from a one-room dwelling, where our girls slept on a concrete floor, to a home where they all have beds. We have done a major wharf cleanup on Rokupa Wharf, created classes and enrichment programs for our children in Ghana, and met basic needs for our children in Uganda for the past five years. We have personally delivered nearly 2,500 "Little Books of Be..." to children in Rwanda, Kenya, Uganda, Sierra Leone, and Ghana. I know this is just the beginning of the work that I will continue to do on the continent of Africa and beyond.

What I have learned from my travels to Africa is to be profoundly grateful for every blessing that I have been given. The people I have met there have been generous, loving, and kind to a stranger. They share the little they have, not knowing where their next meal is coming from, because their generosity comes from their hearts. They dance and they sing, and they live every moment enjoying the little things, because those little things turn out to be the big things in our lives. I no longer sweat the inconveniences of life the way I used to, because I know that there are so many that would be so grateful to have the things that I complain about. My entire being has been transformed because of faith, love, and hope.

The only way I can understand having that vision of that PVC pipe in that grayish-brown wall is from something greater than what I can explain in our physical existence. I was given that image because the Divine already knew what I was called to do here on this earth. There were seeds planted from the time I was a little girl. I am so grateful that I listened to my heart and my soul when I embarked on the unknown, because my life is much better for it. I get to live in the knowledge that there are children around the world that have breathed easier because I have existed, and I believe that is what we are all here to do .

Dawn Airhart Witte

Be the change you wish to see in the world is one of Dawn Airhart Witte's mottos. The Award-Winning Humanitarian,

Author, and Speaker holds many titles, but her proudest is being a mom. A mother will always "be" the nurturing figure in the lives of their children, even when they become adults.

Dawn is the author of seven books including Be..., a collection of reminders of who we can all choose to be in the world. Her book won "The Book Excellence Award" in 2022 and landed on the Amazon Best Seller list. Dawn's "Little Book of Be," a children's version of her Be... book, has been given to over 2,500 children in six different countries in Africa. Dawn is also one of the hosts of The Soulful Conversations Podcast with Portia Booker and Natashah Khan. The podcast features global thought leaders from around the world and discusses how to handle life's greatest challenges.

Dawn has created The Secrets of Being courses and community to help others live happy and fulfilling lives of purpose and passion using her expertise in spirituality, psychology, and humanitarianism.

Prior to following her passion to improve the world, Dawn held a number of leadership positions. She served as PTA President, NCL-LA Founder Chapter President, Court Appointed Special Advocate (CASA), Big Sister, Public Works Commissioner for the City of La Cañada Flintridge, and many others. She attended Cornell University and earned a certification in Animal Assisted Therapies from Harcum College. Dawn recently received an Honorary Doctorate in Humanitarianism from the Global International Alliance. She was the 2021 Women of Achievement Ms. Elite Southern California titleholder. Through each experience, she has learned a great deal about leadership and the importance of inspiring people to greatness. She also serves as an honorary member of the Della Leaders Club and was recently awarded the "100 Most Successful Women in Business" award by the Success Women in Business and the Global Trade Chamber. She is a teacher with the Academy of Divine Knowledge.

Dawn has been a speaker for The Collaborative International Women's Conference hosted by Dr. Gloria Walton. Her work was also spotlighted in Enspire Magazine. Dawn continues to share her message of inspiration and hope by appearing on podcasts and shows around the world.

"Never be afraid to trust an unknown future to a known God."

Corrie ten Boom

Chapter 2

Patrick Meniboon... Doubt to Impact: Self-Belief is Overrated

The Reluctant Valedictorian

"I am not going to speak, and you cannot make me."

Those were the shocking fighting words that I uttered to Dr. Louise C. York, my high school principal in Liberia, when she tried to use her authority to make me give a speech at my graduation.

You see, a day earlier, I was named the valedictorian of the graduating class, and now I had to meet with her since I was absent from school on the day of the announcement.

Have you ever had a feeling that something was about to happen for you, but it would come with a catch? Well, that is what happened.

I intentionally skipped class that day because I had a hunch that morning that I might graduate as one of the two top students. The thought excited me, but it also made me sick to my stomach to think that I might have to give a speech. I decided to skip the graduation, starting with the announcement.

I never imagined that I'd be selected as valedictorian. It had crossed my mind, but since I stuttered, I always thought someone else would be better suited for the role. However, I convinced myself that this was something that I could live with.

Like a lot of people who stutter, I developed what seemed like an effective strategy of avoidance and saying no, even to things I wanted. When it came to being asked to take on leadership roles like class or club president, I would always come up with excuses to get out of the responsibility, or I'd settle for a more behind-the-scenes role such as secretary. Now, something told me that my strategy was about to catch up to me.

So when my roommates and classmates, James Whear and Jeremiah "Ray" Parker, returned from school celebrating me, I knew I had brought it all upon myself; this time, I didn't get asked if I would like to be the valedictorian, I essentially made the decision myself by having earned the highest GPA.

My life of avoidance is infested with a lot of regrets due to missed opportunities, could haves, and should haves; skipping school is another one of those regrets that I have lived with for years. This day should have been my fifteen minutes of fame. I could have basked in the glory of the announcement and the celebration of my overall accomplishment, but I was a no-show on my big day.

Do you know that feeling when you doubt your favorite sports team will win against a formidable opponent, so you don't bother to watch the game, but you immediately want to replay the game after learning the score and discovering that your team had actually won? That's how I felt. I wish I had gone to school for the announcement. This reminds me of another big no-show moment in my life that also still haunts me: I skipped my graduation in middle school, where I was also the valedictorian. As they say, regrets come with no expiration date.

What was supposed to be a proud celebratory moment of accomplishment for me and my joyful friends turned into panic and dread that I not only had to go meet with Mother York, as she was affectionately called, but I also had to give a speech.

Our paths had indirectly crossed before, but never had it been anything close to a one-on-one meeting. I didn't think she even knew who I was. Outwardly, I appeared confident and assured, but inside, I was a trembling mess.

As I approached her office, I remember being in a cold sweat, as if someone had turned on a faucet and drenched me. My heart was pounding so loudly that I was afraid she could hear it from outside the door.

The Meeting

"You do realize that the valedictorian has to give a speech, right?" she asked. I didn't answer her, but I knew my silence was an answer.

Mother York was no taller than 4'10", but she towered in stature, and her reputation as a distinguished educator (and disciplinarian) in Liberia made her seem like she was 7'10" and intimidating. Mother York was "Mama who took no mess." Mother York's no-nonsense approach to discipline and education earned her the respect of many across Liberia. I found her intimidating from afar, and now I had to meet with her one-on-one.

At our meeting, after stuttering my way through some small talks, I told Dr. York that I would be skipping the graduation and, therefore, I would not be speaking. If you had been in the office, you would have seen the shock on both of our faces.

I had even shocked myself when those words slipped out of my trembling, stuttering lips. Being in Dr. York's office was intimidating enough, yet here I was challenging her like a teenager standing up to a feared parent, being rebellious for the first time and wondering within himself whether this was real or an out-of-body experience.

The shock on Mother York's face turned into a smile, as if she was thinking, "Never before has this happened in all my years as principal of this school, you are not going to be the first. This is not going to happen under my watch."

Initially, she tried to use her authority as the principal to change my mind, but she quickly realized my mind was made up and that I was willing to accept my fate if there were consequences that followed my decision.

So she pivoted. She went from being the principal to acting as a mother reassuring a child who needed a hug and some words of encouragement.

At what was the most important time in my young life, I had no relatives around—no father, no mother, nobody! I had no relationship with my dad, and the civil war had divided Liberia along warring faction lines, with families displaced or caught behind the various warring lines, much like East and West Germany during the Cold War.

Five years earlier, my mother had to flee Liberia due to what I call "tribal-political" tension and seek refuge in the United States, but she couldn't take me with her. Up to that point, I don't remember how stuttering fit into my life, but in my new life without my mother, I became self-conscious; I am a stutterer afterall. I struggled severely to cope with living without my mom around. She was the glue that held everything together. The glue had even held my speech together, because until then, I had forgotten that I had a stutter. It seems like along with her own departure, my mother also took my self-confidence, self-belief, and self-image. In her wake, she left lots and lots of fear and insecurities about stuttering. My stutter got debilitatingly worse as I struggled to find myself, my voice, and my confidence.

So now, who better to be a mother figure for me? Dr. York saw the fear I had on my face. She reminded me how far I had come, how proud I should be of myself, and how I would regret skipping graduation. She told me what it would mean not only for myself, but also for the world, if they didn't hear what I had to say.

Has someone ever said the right things to you at the right time? So much so that you thought they had a direct line with your spirit? That's what Mother York did for me.

It was as if I somehow spiritually revealed my story to Dr. York, and she was going to do whatever it took to help me overcome my fear and stuttering: a fear that had held me back from being and feeling like a deserving winner.

Mother York gave me the reassurance that I so desperately needed.

Be Unmesswithable

Almost 25 years to the day after my high school graduation, I walked onto a stage in Nashville, Tennessee, USA, in April 2018 at the PMI Symposium, officially as a professional speaker paid to give a keynote in front of an audience of over 500 people. The audience included a project manager with a lisp who was inspired to pursue his dream of becoming a John Maxwell Certified Speaker (I checked and verified that he got certified).

Only 3 years earlier in 2015, I was announced as a district finalist at the Toastmasters International Contest, one contest win away from qualifying for the World Championship of Public Speaking, having defeated a 3-time qualifier in the process. For me, a guy who is always defined by his stutter, this is one of the top 10% of accomplishments in my life. It has everything to do with redefining my self-image, mastering my courage, and standing up to the bully of stuttering. Do you know how they say a rising tide raises all boats? I know of no other skill that is capable of this kind of transformation on several levels than public speaking. Secretly, between you and me, public speaking is my way of taking on something that most of the world fears. Selfishly, it is my Toby Keith "How Do You Like Me Now" moment.

What is your own "How Do You Like Me Now" moment?

What may have been your story of devastation, loss, and a life filled with self-pity can turn into a story of grit, unwavering resilience, and mastering courage as a primary source of psychological fuel.

I know you also want to find out what happened to that reluctant valedictorian. Well, I will tell you later. For now, your own story is waiting to be told!

Doubt is just a signal that something in your life needs your attention; it does not have to define you.

If you are not telling your story, you are holding up the line of people waiting on you before they get started on their journey. You are holding up more than just yourself.

The world is waiting to SEE your voice!

To your Unmesswithable Courage!

Patrick Meniboon

Patrick Meniboon is known as The Courage Hacker. He is a strategist and speaker who helps professionals, especially those with speech impediments, bridge the gap between their doubt and impact by upgrading their self-image and mastering courage.

From a high school class valedictorian who attempted to skip his graduation because of his stutter to a 2015 District Finalist in the Toastmasters International Speech Contest, one win away from qualifying for the World Championship of Public Speaking, Patrick has battled against doubt and fear, and walked the talk on mastering courage to become a voice on self-mastery.

Patrick is the author of the upcoming book, *Unmesswithable: How I Got Paid To Stutter In Public*, which chronicles his journey from overcoming self-doubt to becoming a successful public speaker and provides readers with a blueprint for overcoming their own version of stuttering.

Father of two, Rachel and Lance, Patrick originally comes from Liberia and now lives in the Raleigh area of North Carolina, in the United States.

In his spare time, Patrick enjoys playing tennis, copywriting, and admiring and collecting belt buckles (he has quite the collection).

Patrick can be found online at patrickmeniboon.com.

"Sometimes beautiful things come into our lives out of nowhere. We can't always understand them, but we have to trust in them. I know you want to question everything, but sometimes it pays to just have a little faith."

Lauren Kate

Chapter 3

Laura Brennan Ballet...The Empowerment of Believing

When I was fourteen years old, I vividly remember sitting in a beam of sunlight, nestled in a big comfy chair, somehow aware of my surroundings from a different perspective than ever before. I was, in that moment, connecting to the beginning of what would be a lifelong exploration into the journey of self-empowerment. What was missing at a young age was the ability to BELIEVE in myself. It has taken what seems like a lifetime to advance my mind and allow the frequency of connectivity within my body to catch up with the accelerated process of believing in myself.

When we align with this knowing—whether through our faith, our belief in our own consciousness, or simply allowing ourselves to go outside of our own doing—we begin to resonate with a higher power; here in this expansion, beyond self, is where we begin to believe in a power that elevates our existence. The beautiful alchemy of our universe is that she provides us with this glorious experience; when we believe in something, it will then manifest. However, for most of us, we place repetitive thinking into that old adage: we must first see something in order to then believe it exists.

Aha, Grasshopper, herein lies the journey of an enlightened soul. In order to believe in something, or in someone, one must first go within and find that personal connection to self. This is not a selfish act of being—quite the opposite. This is the act of servitude, for when we know ourselves, we then can begin to heal the collective. If we don't authentically believe in ourselves, which we discover through this most important relationship, we cannot then ask of another to believe. To believe is an inside journey. To believe is to know, without doubt, without any obstruction, that first we must believe it to be true, and then we will see its unfolding into a manifested state.

It is when times of challenge arise in our daily life that both the test and the resolve of the authenticity of true belief can be created. It is within the contrast of dark and light, negative and positive, belief and doubt, where the true nature of believing releases its most reflective state: the experience of knowing that something exists without seeing its existence.

When an obstacle arises, fear can settle in, and here is where we need to connect with the belief that we have what is needed to not only manage the negativity of the challenge, but to believe in ourselves, and to know that we can advance through to a positive outcome. Here, we can begin to gain new insights, gather wisdom, and learn new skills; in doing so, we gain an internal support system, so when the next challenge arises, we are prepared. I have found that when I have experienced pain, sadness, or frustration, when I am in the middle of a hurricane of stress, as long as I connect to what I believe in, I can be at the gateway of calm.

It can take decades for some of us to begin to merge into a relationship with what "believing" means, as it is such a shared—yet personal—experience. When we are at our most vulnerable, it helps to connect to a system of unwavering support. Faith in that higher connection allows us to handle challenges with grace and to feel less alone, even when we really are alone. Here in this vast, yet intimate, space of survival is where I have cultivated what I personally believe in. For each individual, a relationship of connection with a higher power is a deep and personal journey. I feel this is the true journey of champions: connecting to the unseen and untouchable, and knowing that we have within ourselves the ability to create what it means to BELIEVE IN.

I have chosen to connect to a belief system that takes my mindset into the exploration of never saying never. All things are possible. Who am I to proclaim what another human being should or should not believe in? I find it a beautiful and empowering trait that humans possess the ability to think for ourselves—to explore and expand on new knowledge, new insights, and, at times, ancient teachings. Human beings retain the God-given right to grow, to flourish, and to create new ways of navigating through hardships and downfalls. Our faith, our belief, that we are not alone in this world is how we elevate as a compassionate civilization.

I have been asked the question, "If you could go back into childhood and do something differently, what would you do?" One of the fundamental skills I wish I had acquired early in my youth would be to believe in my potential and the ability to see that potential into fruition. I've noticed throughout all my Life Empowerment Coaching, world speaking engagements, and Global New Thought Leadership discussions, most adults wish they had had a super power back in their youth that would have released them from the unnecessary history of regret. If we had connected to the confidence of our potential and all that we are capable of creating, our lives certainly would have turned out differently. The beautiful thing is that we can begin to believe in anything we want to, at any time, and recalibrate the present environment.

If we believed in human potential—the actual experience of fulfilling our potential—we would begin to understand that we are here, in physical form, with a mind that has no limits. The only limitations we place upon ourselves are the beliefs of our own self- doubt. Wherever we place our faith, we are all connected: one community, one world. Each of our actions as an individual has the power to either create a negative effect or a positive effect upon the collective environment. We all have the same access to the opportunity to evolve in this lifetime, and when awareness of this opportunity presents itself, you must believe it. Create a life of happiness.

This is where the lack of believing in oneself comes into play all too often. A while ago, I was faced with a life-changing heartbreak. I did not see it coming; as for most of us, we rarely do. I reacted rather than responded, and despite decades of collecting wisdom, merging with loving insights, and gaining mastery over a high-level skill set, I found doubt creeping in. The coping mechanism that was in place was outdated. I was questioning my belief.

When the thought of not believing in my own personal philosophy came rushing in, it was an opportunity to reconnect deeper into what I have always known. I immediately went to my training within The Science of Empowerment. I once again studied the J3=E Formula, and applied the five principles of human advancement. I remembered why we are here: to expand the mind, to connect to our faith, to observe the spiritual energy moving within us, and to believe once more in the knowledge that we are not alone, and we can persevere.

Challenges, hardships, and life lessons come at us for many reasons, and at times that seem off balance to the flow of life. Here, in the atmosphere of a neutral mind, I believed that I could move myself through this ordeal, because I have studied the mapping system of belief within myself.

Though we may all use a different language of expression, and at times, we may feel our personal chosen faith is somehow better or on a higher plane then another, the universal knowing that we truly are all connected is a common agreement. Though we, as a global family, experience distortion and negativity, there are examples of leadership that remind us of how united we can be.

We want to believe that there is magic and power outside of ourselves. However, for some of us, connecting to a higher purpose and placing the belief in a higher presence brings peace and resolve to many of the unanswerable questions we can, at times, face.

It does not personally matter to me what someone believes in. I love the passion and the connectivity to the act of believing in something, period! You can worship a butterfly and I would think that is a beautiful experience to have. Whether you believe first in another power, or you first believe in the power of self, either way, you are connecting to the universal flow of connectivity.

Sometimes we need to put our trust in a higher power in order to move us through an event, a condition, a loss. When we suffer, the belief in a reason for the pain helps in the process of healing. This trust can empower us and carry the weight and the hurt away. I will always remain in faith, and believe in the goodness and the compassion of humanity.

Stay connected to your principles and design a beautiful life. Never waver from what you know is your truth and your journey. Remain steadfast and strong and be in service to others as often as possible. Lead by example, as this is an authentic way of being, and live an empowered life through believing that you were born for greatness.

Laura Brennan Ballet

As the Author of "The Science of Empowerment," Laura is driven by the life force that circulates within all universal connectivity. Her passion, motivation, and ability to see how energy is in everything, guides her powerful messaging forward. When you are in connection with Laura, you feel the charge and the movement of energy in real-time.

This energy comes alive and sparks an awareness within, uplifting thought and purpose for the observer. Laura's energetic ability, through her words, to activate within the listener the personal knowing that they are living potentiality is inspiring.

As an Ambassador of Life Empowerment, a global top-selling author, a New Thought Creator, an Energy Alignment Coach, and a Zielo Corporate Coach, Laura's exploration forward into the awakening of global potential is at the foundation of her mission.

When you are in connection with the knowledge that Laura provides, you become empowered. As you begin to witness your own authenticity and recognition into your individualized state of genius, an awakening to your personal brilliance advances.

It is essential to the human condition that we remember why it is that we are here, and that is to evolve.

Laura's mission and legacy is to create an energetic connection to the new sciences of knowledge, and to activate a higher understanding within the human community. We are destined to live a life of happiness, positivity, and purpose. "The Science of Empowerment," if you are willing, will begin your journey into self-evolution; here, in this exploration of connectivity, is where empowerment is created.

www.linkedin.com/in/laura-brennan-ballet-bb426751

https://www.instagram.com/thescienceofempowerment/

https://www.facebook.com/laura.brennan.56614/

https://www.youtube.com/channel/UCsBfQy8Sp78NZIZ9Q-OqrMg

https://thescienceofempowerment.com/

https://www.facebook.com/laurabballet/

"None of us knows what might happen even the next minute, yet still we go forward. Because we trust. Because we have faith."

Paul Coelho

Chapter 4
Louise Bieshke... Kentucky to California 2003

When we go on vacation, my husband, Patrick, and I plan the entire trip, because we have already decided where we are going and how long we are going to stay to enjoy the area. But what would we do if we were thinking about moving to another state, starting a whole new life across the country? It is not the same as a vacation; we were planning on living in a new area for a long time. Welcome, September 2003!

Looking at each and every room in the house and seeing all the furniture, the pictures hanging on the walls, the clothes in the closets, the dishes in the cabinets, and all the stuff in the garage besides our cars made my head swim! Wow, this wasn't going to be easy.

We loved our hometown of Lexington, Kentucky, but both of us had seen other family members move to other states, and they seemed to love their new lives. We were ready to join those folks who ventured out of their comfort zones; for us, that meant starting to experience California by moving to Los Angeles.

The excitement of wanting to move to Los Angeles, California, kept growing and growing, as we knew we would be getting new jobs, looking for a place to live, and getting to be close to at least one of our children and his family. We have three sons and a daughter, and they all have families—except Joe, who now lives in heaven.

Driving a U-HAUL truck with a car attached to the back on a trailer did not scare us, as we had each other to depend on for conversation, for driving time, for looking out for places to eat and stay, and for areas to park this long truck with our whole physical life packed in it! I think the fear didn't set in until we were halfway across the country, somewhere in Arkansas. I began wondering, "Are we doing the right thing?"

Patrick reassured me in a few ways during our conversations: he had always been successful in achieving goals he set, and we were educated and passionate people who loved life. We weren't wealthy, but had always made sure we had food on the table, clothes on our backs, and a little something put aside for emergencies. Wouldn't that be true wherever we lived? Wouldn't we strive for the same values and comforts in California as we had in Kentucky? Our adult children were not dependent on us, and we were ready for a new adventure.

But wanting and striving for life's goals versus actually making them happen is not as easy as it can sound in a conversation or written on paper. Having to drive in California traffic, finding a new church, making new friends, and making enough money to pay our bills were prominent fears of mine. Of course, there are bigger fears in life, but we have to tackle the minute-by-minute, day-by-day, month-by-month and year-by-year concerns, right? We had already experienced one of the biggest challenges in a way no parent ever wants to imagine—the death of a child. I found myself ready to embrace the tasks ahead of us.

I had a genuine interest in finding employment. It is not hard for me to be considerate of the feelings of others, and a dose of patience in looking for a new home rewarded Patrick and I with a delightful house we then continued to live in for the next 13 years.

Patrick and I live faith-based lives, so one might think we would be praying to find safety in our travels, to secure good jobs, and to settle into our new city comfortably. However, I learned in 1986, when our son Joe died, that praying for specific requests to God is not how prayer works for me. Yes, prayer is communication with God, but when I start praying for specific things, I need to take a moment and pray that whatever happens, God is with me through it all. God was with my family when Joe was healthy and when he was sick. God gave Patrick and me strong and loving friends and family, resilient children, the capacity to think about what to do next, and the ability to depend on those people who would be there for us for the rest of our lives. I didn't realize at the time of Joe's suffering at 16 years old that my prayers for him to get well, or for me to take his place and die so that he may live, that God really was with me. I thought He deserted my family. It was only when someone said, "God is just as sorry that Joe died as you are," did I feel that God was trying to comfort me through this person. God knows All because He created this world we live in, but He is not a magician who waves a magic wand. I was praying for a specific desire and outcome. I have read in the bible, in poems, and in other books and articles that we die to live eternally. I have had to face other deaths of loved ones, and I began to feel more and more that the statement was true. Now I don't just read it, I feel it and believe it. Death brings with it a whole range of emotions, struggles, and, eventually, acceptance, and the ability to move forward one "breathe-in-and-breathe-out" at a time.

Since 1986, I have found that seeking out self-help books, like *When Bad Things Happen to Good People* by Harold Kushner, gives me a sense of not being alone in my struggles. Going to the library, I am drawn to the self-help book section. Sometimes I don't buy anything, but if something speaks to me, I pick it up and consider its worth. People who are willing to share their struggles, opinions, successes, and failures are sharing real-life situations. It is not fiction. I have used suggestions I have found in others' writings, like allowing myself to feel terrible, to cry, to sleep, to put off a task until the next day, to have fun, and to realize everything isn't going to fix itself immediately.

On prayer cards I have, I see the words, "humbly ask," "courage," "from the heart," "live forever in peace and good will," and "Amen." A cheerful word is nice to hear, but sometimes others are not in a happy place, like on the freeway; being generous with praise motivates people, but what if they had just found out they lost their job? Being alert to a friend's needs is what can count most in some situations, but most of the time I am solving my own problems.

When I think about the challenges Patrick and I faced in getting new jobs, looking for a place to live, making new friends, and finding a new church, I remember pulling into Redondo Beach and looking forward to seeing our son and family there. Mark's extended family welcomed us by having us over for meals, helping us find a realtor to start looking for a house, and inviting us to gatherings with food, games, fun conversation, and hugs when we entered. And they didn't just stop at hugs when we left, they would walk us to our car to see us off safely. The Filipino traditions and hospitality of our extended family only increased our vision of "this is going to be a good place to have a good living." California provided for us diversity, a multitude of employment options, new friends, new challenges, and new ways of solving problems.

Life is victory and defeat; it is about rebounding. The greatest lesson I learned from our California adventure is to accept the sunshine and the rain. Both can be abundant or scarce.

It's heartwarming to look to the sky and think Joe is there somewhere.

It's fun to smile.

It's okay to enjoy a chocolate chip cookie.

It's nice to watch our children and their families love each other.

It's okay to move to another state and start a new life!

LOUISE BIESCHKE

Louise Bieschke lives in Houston, Texas, with her husband, Patrick. She likes to read, mow the yard, plant flowers that will live, and try to appreciate the humid summer weather of Texas. Winter months remind her of California weather, so they are much more fun for taking walks, sitting on the back porch, and opening the windows for a breeze to sneak in the house. When not outside, Louise likes to cook, bake, and watch PBS NewsHour.

Louise volunteers at Holy Ghost Catholic Church in the choir, while Patrick participates as a lector or Eucharistic Minister at Mass. Louise and Patrick volunteer at Gulf Coast Regional Blood Center.

Louise is appreciative of all the technology we have now, so FaceTimes with family in California, Kentucky, Oregon, North Carolina, Pennsylvania, Florida, Utah, Virginia, Georgia, Ohio, Indiana, and New York take place on a regular basis. Texas family and friends interact with Louise in person!

Louise retired after working for CASA of Los Angeles in Monterey Park, CA. Working with volunteers who help children in foster care find permanency filled an important part of her life with joy and respect for people who are willing to give of their time and talents to make a difference in what a child's future could look like.

Growing up in Lexington, Kentucky; marrying Patrick Bieschke; and having four children, eight grandchildren, and exceptional daughters-in-law and a son-in-law are blessings Louise thanks God for every day.

You can contact Louise at louisebieschke@yahoo.com

"Once the seed of faith takes root, it cannot be blown away, even by the strongest wind. Now that's a blessing."

Rumi

Chapter 5
Bulasio Bulumo... The Story of Buluma Bulasio

I'm Buluma Bulasio, an orphan who lives at Mama Josephine's orphanage in Busia, Uganda, East Africa. I take this chance to write my biography that whoever reads it takes heart.

I lost my parents when I was three and my little sister was two years old. My sister was named Selina. When we lost our parents, we started living with an old woman who was in her 80s. She was so old that she couldn't even support herself.

She later handed us to the nearby church in the village in Sibara where we started living. After some time, we came to meet Mama Josephine, who was a widow and a member of our church. Mama had lost her children in the war of Lakwena. Since she was a member of the church, the pastor knew that she had a passion for loving and taking care of the orphans; that's the only job that she wanted to do in her entire life. She carried us to her home, and we started living with her. Mama Josephine used to work in the food market where she would go work, and in return she would collect some grains to help us survive and support us with some school fees in the primary level. She collected beans and maize, which we later also ground to get flour for us to eat. We started as a small family, but as I talk of now, we are 65 orphans, some of us were street kids, and others were abandoned by their parents. We struggle to get food to eat, school fees, and also health care. This is a big challenge for Mama Josephine.

As I speak of now, I still need more support to help me go through my university studies for a Bachelor's Degree in Textiles and Apparel Design. I want to become a fashion star in the future. I want to design for the entire world so that it looks colorful. When I finish my studies, I will also help orphans who are going through the same situation I went through.

I faced a challenge of not staying with my biological parents, but as I talk of now, I really feel like I have them since Mama Josephine came into my life. Mama is really a blessing to my life. I also have another miracle who is a parent to every person in this world, and that's Mama Dawn Witte. I really love her because she came as a blessing to my life. She is so inspiring and encouraging. I wish everyone would be like her. Then we would conquer this world through being kind to one another.

There are many challenges that I face still to this day, but I believe in the Almighty Father. With Him everything is possible. I struggled with my high school, I used to play football to help support myself academically and with scholastic materials. But that is no longer an option because there is a lot of segregation in football associations in Uganda, and at my level it can't take me anywhere.

I lived in bad conditions where you could not go beg for something from the neighborhood because each homestead could only mind their own business.

I had a fear of living a permanent life which was so miserable since I was an orphan; it would make me cry because I didn't have hopes of being what I am now, even though I am still hustling through life.

I praise almighty God for that.

My other fear was to become a failure at an early age. That is one of the common fears that no one wishes to have. It is so embarrassing to fail at a young age without having gone to school to get some knowledge and skills.

This was due to lack of enough funds to help me pay school fees. Imagine having nothing to eat at home, and yet you want money for school fees. I feared living a miserable life of suffering.

I was so sad and thought that I would not be what I am today, though I still need a hand to successfully reach my destination. At my young age I experienced suffering because I had lost hope of everything.

Wanting to be loved and taken care of as any other child was killing me slowly because I would see other happy families and I admired them because they were a family.

My faith got me through by being a God-fearing person, and it taught me to love, ease, and support others, to always be obedient and always have God within me. God has a plan for everyone, and our conditions are not permanent in this world.

I served the devil through being God-fearing because since my childhood, I learned my post and have always had a dream of being someone important, just like Mama Josephine loved me and takes care of those in need.

I believe in sharing the little that I have with someone who is in need of it, because if you want to wait until you get enough before you share with someone, then you will never actually have enough. Even the bible says to share the little you have, and God shall open for you the blessings for more.

Respect for everyone is also a key to success, because through respect you can get new friends who uplift you.

The greatest lesson I have learned is that life is a continuous learning experience. Throughout our lives we keep rising and falling, learning important lessons along the way.

I shall always walk my path which will drive me to my final destination, because there are people who will always judge you and will try to curve for your future.

Good things don't come easy, of course. If you want to have a good life with a successful career, live a trustworthy life. If I rushed into something bad in my early age, it would have ruined my life.

Make good friends who can support you and will always be there for you in times that you need them.

Never lose hope, because God has a plan for everyone, and no condition is permanent.

Believe in Him and be patient. In time, He will answer your call.

Never fail to try, because even an athlete could lead the entire race only to fall just in front of the finish line and lose.

Never regret anything that has happened in your life because it cannot be changed, undone, or forgotten. Take everything as a lesson learned and move on with life.

BULUMA BULASIO

Bulasio is a talented footballer and football is his passion. He has won many medals and certificates.

He is a student at Kyambogo University in Kampala Uganda, pursuing a Bachelor's Degree in Textile and Apparel Design. He is currently in his second year of a three year program.

Bulasio wants to become a famous fashion designer in this world. That is his goal in the future. He also wants to inspire the young generation and the elderly people in this world. He wants to work with professional designers all over the continents. He is inspired and encouraged by Mom Dawn because he believes she is such an inspiration in this world.

His dream is to mentor those who don't have opportunities and help them be important people in this world.

You can connect with Bulasio at:

Yahoo   bulumabulasio@yahoo.com

Facebook   Basho B Bruce

WhatsApp   +256 788342145

Thank you all so much. I love you all and may God bless you abundantly.

"On a long journey of human life, faith is the best of companions; it is the best refreshment on the journey; and it is the greatest property."

Buddha

CHAPTER 6

Father Jean d'Amor... God's Love and Forgiveness Have No Limits

May the spirit of Ubuntu help us to be the imitators of God!

"Mercy will always be greater than any sin, no one can place limits on the love of God who is ever ready to forgive." – Pope Francis, Misericordiae Vultus, n. 3

I have been very touched by these words, recalling how God has always shown his mercy towards human beings throughout the ages. He never tires of forgiving us, even when we tire of asking him for forgiveness and mercy.

Mercy is another name for God: he is naturally a merciful Father. He cannot *not* forgive us. Therefore, there is no sin that he can't forgive. He showed his mercy first when he created human beings out of his merciful love, and his purpose is to give us his own life. His mercy goes beyond anything that can keep us away from that life, including our sins and our lack of faith in him, because he loves all of us unconditionally. God always seeks to save us, and his heart is restless until we all are saved. No one can place limits on his love towards each human being. Instead, we all are called to be his "accomplices" in order to bring about his salvation to each of his children. The best way to collaborate with God is to bear witness to his love and forgiveness.

However, we fail to imitate him because of our weakness. We tire of forgiving, we tire even of asking for forgiveness. God encourages us to forgive without counting how many times our neighbor has trespassed against us (cf. Mt 18:21-22). We must learn to forgive as God has forgiven us: "If you, Lord, kept a record of sins, Lord, who could stand?" (Ps 130:3). These words invite us to be humble and avoid judging others when they fall down and sin, because we all are sinners who have been forgiven. However, we must also accept our limits. We are not God. We should forgive others because they are not God, either. When we fail to be like God, we ask him to do the good we have failed to accomplish.

This insight makes me reflect on the words of Christ on the cross: "Father, forgive them, because they do not know what they are doing" (Lk 23:34). These words are very powerful. The betrayal that Jesus experienced was so enormous that it may have gone beyond his understanding. Humanly speaking, for him, it may have seemed hard to forgive. However, he knew that his Father was always ready to forgive even an unforgivable sin. Sometimes we are so grieved that it becomes very hard—even seemingly impossible—to forgive, but our Father is always ready to forgive what we fail to forgive. His mercy is always greater than any sin. Jesus is a perfect example to imitate.

The words of Christ on the cross constitute an invitation to entrust ourselves to God whenever we struggle in forgiving those who trespass against us. God needs just one word that shows our good will to forgive, then he does the rest. We only need to give him an "opportunity," so that through our good will he can forgive: "Whatever you loose on earth will be loosed in heaven" (Mt 16:19).

When I fail to forgive, do I remember that God has forgiven me? When I feel that the pain caused by my neighbor is too heavy to be forgiven, do I remember that God's mercy has no limits? Do I remember to ask God to forgive what I am failing to forgive?

Another secret to forgiveness is to remember our real identity. The more we remember who truly we are, the more we will be open to forgiveness, because we will realize that those who harm us are our brothers and sisters with whom we share the same essence of being human beings.

That is the spirit of Ubuntu, the African philosophy that emphasizes our "oneness and interconnectedness." Ubuntu means "I am because you are." If I deny your "being," I deny mine as well. I deny my Ubuntu. My humanity is so inextricably bound up in the humanity of each human being that when I dehumanize others, I dehumanize myself. In my mother tongue, we believe that only God possesses Ubuntu in its fullness, and we also name him Nyir'ubuntu: the One who has Ubuntu in fullness, the One from whom Ubuntu comes and flows towards human beings. In God's Ubuntu, we believe that he is tender and merciful, never causing us to suffer or experience wrath. Therefore, a person of Ubuntu imitates Nyir'ubuntu by treating others with Ubuntu (humanity) and compassion. A person of Ubuntu forgives as Nyir'ubuntu does.

Forgiveness is an act of Ubuntu, because it gives back to the offenders what they had lost while treating others as if they were less human. At a certain level in their sufferings, victims believe that their offenders have lost their humanity, and thus, could make them suffer. Offenders harm us when they forget about our shared real identity, and by offending us, they not only deny our humanity, but they also dehumanize themselves, going astray from their own identity. However, in their mind, they believe that they are showing how powerful they are to their victims. We should know that we are only powerful when we strive to lift up our fellow human beings—even our enemies—bringing them back to their "real selves." When the victims come to forgive, they see again the offenders as human beings who had forgotten who they truly are. The more we recognize our shared Ubuntu with offenders, the more we will forgive them; moved by pity for them, we will realize that the offenders did wrong to us by the ignorance of who they essentially are: *abantu*, or human beings. We only affirm our humanity when we recognize the humanity of others and treat them as we would like them to treat us. This idea reminds me of a powerful verse of a poem written by a genocide survivor in Rwanda: "If you really knew me and you really know yourself, you would not have killed me." The ignorance of our real selves can lead to such atrocities as genocide. The awareness of our Ubuntu inspires us to be "God-like."

Prayer: O merciful God, Nyir'ubuntu, you never tire of forgiving my sins and the sins of the world. Your mercy goes beyond my betrayals and failures. You don't count my sins. Instead, you cause my efforts to change and become better, and you bestow your mercy upon me. O Lord, give me the courage to forgive my brothers and sisters without counting how many times they have trespassed against me. I would like to be a forgiving person, as you are. If I face something that is hard to forgive, fill my heart with your light, so that I may remember that you can forgive what seems to be unforgivable. In such circumstances, I want to imitate your Son and, like him, say: "Father, forgive them, because they don't know what they are doing." Amen.

Jean d'Amour Dusengumuremyi is a Catholic priest from Rwanda, in Byumba Diocese. In addition to his passion for preaching the Good News of Jesus Christ, Fr. Jean d'Amour feels very concerned about the duty of memory and has published books on Felicite Niyitegeka, one of the great heroes of Rwanda who willingly gave their lives while protecting Tutsi during the genocide in 1994. In 2014, he "discovered" the philosophy of Ubuntu, and since then, he became eager to spread it through sharing and writings.

JEAN D'AMOUR DUSENGUMUREMYI

"I think believing in something is what matters most. Believe in nature or believe in love or believe that by doing the right thing you can make some difference to another human being or an entire generation."

Rachel C. Weingarten

CHAPTER 7

NATASHAH KHAN... HOW I CAME TO BELIEVE

I was desperate. I had lost it all: my mind, my identity, my marriage, my spouse, my kids, my house, I lost it all. I attempted suicide with the desire to end it once and for all, because I had no hope, no courage; I was buried in guilt, shame, fear, and despair. As far as I was concerned, my life was over after almost 13 years of marriage that ended due to infidelity, secrets, lies, distrust, and emotional disconnect. I had failed as a wife, mother, daughter, sister; I had failed in life. My thought was a question, "What is there left to live for?! No one loves me, I am not good enough, I am a failure!" At that time, I had fallen so far into the depths of darkness, I couldn't see beyond my present circumstances. I couldn't, or didn't, want to hear that all that I had worked hard for was lost forever. I didn't have the knowledge or wisdom to understand that everything that was happening, everything and everyone I had lost, was all for a greater purpose; I couldn't see it in that moment. At this point, I was so far removed from reality, from my life, and from any understanding of who or what a higher power or GOD meant. How could there be anything out there that could possibly return me to sanity when I had always thought that I was the one in control of my life and my destiny.

PASSION: Natashah has dedicated her time to healing relationships and is a published author of two virtual articles, "Understanding the Disease of Addiction" and "Victim to Victory." She is also a contributing writer for a virtual magazine, I *Shine Magazine*.

GOAL: Having been a survivor of abuse and in recovery for the last 11 years, Natashah has established EMPOWERED VOICES LLC, where she is a Relational Coach focusing on empowering others to have a voice, to fulfill their life's purpose, and to heal from the wounds that have become disruptive and hindered their ability to live their lives in a fulfilling and meaningful way.

Chapter 8

Bobby Manard... A Rose Between Two Thorns

It was early morning on a cold November day, and you could hear me in the shower crying from a place deep within my heart and soul, pleading with God: "Please, God, please show me a rose today. I need to see a rose between the two major thorns today. I need this to know that you're really here with me, and for me, and guiding me. Please!!!"

You see, later that morning, after I relieved one of my brothers of his time with my dad, it would then be my turn to be alone with dad, and to say my heartfelt goodbyes. He was a few days into his hospice journey, and we were informed that he could be called Home at any time.

As if that wasn't challenging enough, later that day, in the evening, I had a meeting with a mediator to start the process of dissolving my marriage with my best friend, my wife.

So, on the same day, I was essentially saying goodbye to two of the people I loved most in the world. The two losses were two of six major, life-changing losses that would happen virtually concurrently, and these losses cut deeply, especially because my mom had passed in my 20s, so there was no real comfort to be found.

I knew I was especially strong, since I had been dealing with loss after loss after loss, yet I also knew that without God's intervention, the day's events could lead to me doing something disastrous.

I met with Dad, and shared my heartfelt thoughts and tearful goodbyes. Then, when I was ready to leave, for some reason I was delayed a bit because I was flustered and couldn't put my coat on. A few minutes later, as I was heading to the elevator for the parking garage, Intuition said to me, "Take the stairs!" I really didn't want to take the stairs, because I was in a terrible mood, yet Intuition was adamant: "Take the stairs!"

Finally, and reluctantly, I took the stairs to the top floor of the parking garage. I remember looking up and saying sarcastically, "Happy now???" as I was looking up at God.

Within moments, I noticed a woman waving at me, yet I didn't initially recognize her. As she got closer, I recognized her as a friend, a nurse, and one of my early coaching clients. She gave me a big hug and appeared delighted to see me. I could tell by her demeanor and energy that she was having quite the emotional day herself. We chatted for a bit then said our goodbyes.

Then it hit me, as tears were streaming down my face, and my body was trembling while I was walking towards my car. I opened the door and just plopped on my seat and kept crying the deep-seated tears that have only happened rarely, if ever, in my life.

You see, my friend's middle name is Rose. She was the Rose between the two thorns of my most difficult day. I asked God for a rose that day, and God answered my call. I knew then that I would be not only ok, but also that ultimately, I would thrive.

On one of the most difficult days of my life, during the darkest period of my life, I asked God for help, and my prayers were answered. All of my life until then I had been fiercely independent, which, in and of itself, is not necessarily a bad quality, yet it is limiting. On that day, I significantly grew on my journey to being interdependent with Spirit.

Interdependence with Spirit is far more powerful and effective than fierce independence, and it's easy. All you have to do is ask for help and believe, with all your heart, that it will come. That's all I did. I wish I had learned that much earlier in life, yet, back then, my life lessons had only taught me that nobody had my back.

What I didn't realize is that God ALWAYS had my back. Now I know without a doubt. God is, and has ALWAYS been, there for me. The same is true for you. I just hope you don't choose to wait until the most difficult day of your life to understand and live this truth.

As a side note, within the following year of running into my friend, I told her my story. It turns out that I was the rose in her day that day, as it also had been an incredibly difficult day for her. She prayed to God for assistance and for a sign, and I was that sign for her. Interesting how that works. There's so much happening in the unseen world; we just have to truly trust and notice what happens.

So, what about you? Will you consider fully trusting in the Divine Spirit now and for the rest of your life? If so, rest assured that you will consistently enjoy magical experiences in your life!

BOBBY MANARD

Hi! I'm Bobby Manard from *insideout.coach*. I help smart, talented, nice people transform their lives from the Inside Out. I combine the best of the Outside strategies I learned from world-class coaches and leaders, including John Maxwell, Jack Canfield, Jim Camp, and many others. I have numerous certifications including NLP Master Coach and Practitioner, Leadership Coach, Jack Canfield Certified Trainer and Success Principles Coach, Negotiation Coach, and World Class Speaking Coach. As far as the Inside strategies, I am Certified in Spiritual Energy Mastery, as well as a Reiki Master, Master Hypnotherapist, and Master EFT Practitioner. I'm an empath with my own "Dark Night of the Soul" experience informing my personal transformation, as I experienced six major life changes virtually at once. That experience has also greatly enhanced my Intuitive gifts, which allows me to customize solutions for clients using the multi-faceted approach from the Outside, Inside, and Intuitive perspectives. I'm not a therapist, and I'm not just a guy with only book knowledge who has read and/or scanned 10,000 plus books. I've got much more than just book knowledge. I also have the "I don't want to be here knowledge." Having both kinds of knowledge makes me remarkably valuable. Some people have outer credentials. Others have an inner gift. Some have both, and I'm proud to say I have both. I'm an expert with Coaching, Leadership, Negotiation, Mindset, Success Principles, Energy, High Performance, Transformation, Speaking, Storytelling, and more. I believe your life truly matters. Let's make it count, shall we?

"You must not lose faith in humanity. Humanity is like an ocean; if a few drops of the ocean are dirty, the ocean does not become dirty."

Mahatma Gandhi

Chapter 9

Kunle Pelemo... Believe and Just Do It

What do you do when you're about to make a career-shifting decision? It could be tough, especially when you're leaving the "certainty" to pave a new course for yourself. Sometimes the nature and volumes of advice with which you are barraged make it more complicated. Let me lead you into this short story of mine.

From my early years, I have found my purpose in life. I have been a people person and love to lead by serving others. My time in a higher institution presented me with the opportunity to lead in various groups for about three years. I still look back and love how I was able to make a positive impact and touch lives while leading, be it from the back or otherwise. Then I graduated and got a job in one of the busiest sectors in my country: the oil and gas downstream sector. Oil and gas is a mainstay of my nation's economy, so working in that sector comes with its profit and pride. However, in spite of my busy work schedule, I would still find time to squeeze that part of impacting people—both in and out of the workplace—into my new work-life. This could be draining and tiring, maintaining a striking balance between the two.

Being a strategist, it was a bit easier for me in the initial stage of my work experience. But maybe, because of the situation in which I found myself, working for about 12 hours daily and commuting for about 6 hours combined the same day (18 hours in total), it made doing other stuff very difficult. I had people that I mentored, both young and old, coupled with a speaking career I had built while I was in school; all these were beginning to lag. There came an incident that took me to the introductory part of my story where I had to make a critical decision. A decision about quitting my 9-to-5 (oh, I call it 5-to-9) after working for about a decade to face where I found fulfillment. Hey, listen. I am not saying you have to quit your job to find fulfillment. This is about my reality and how I handled it.

My decision to quit my job was fueled by an incident that nearly happened to one of my protégés. This is a story of how my intervention helped prevent her from taking her life (I am choosing not to use the phrase "committing suicide").

She's young, beautiful, creative, and hardworking, and has loads of other qualities that are pointers to her becoming a successful lady. However, life sometimes comes in phases where you might not get your desirable result in the immediate. I never knew she was in that phase. I never knew that sometimes, her struggles and pains were covered in the façade of wide smiles, make-up, and perfumes. I never knew she was at the breaking point. I never knew her response, "I'm fine," when asked how she was doing, did not always reflect her state of mind.

On a fateful day, I got back from work late at night and decided to check on her. I put a call through. "How are you doing?" was my first question. You guessed her reply, right? "I'm fine." I was observant enough to notice a very faint sigh before her response. So I pressed further to ask if she really meant what she said. It didn't take long before her defense was broken. She broke down in tears and lamented how life had been unfair to her and how she gets little or no returns after putting in great efforts in her business. At that point, she paused before confessing she had planned to end it all. In her words, "If I'm gone, at least the pressure will be gone, too."

I was shocked and afraid. This period coincided with the time there was a rise in suicide cases across my country. I knew it was high time I did what I could to help a friend. We spoke at length. I listened to her with empathy. I promised to be part of her support system right then and beyond. It worked. She cried and let out the pressure. The burden was lifted off her heart. I told her some things to do to help her, mentally, and was a constant plug for her whenever she needed someone to talk to. She's alive and doing well, fulfilling her dreams and moving on against all odds.

There and then, it dawned on me that there are millions of people around the world who need something similar to get them off the pang of suicide and other effects of mental health-related issues, starting within my immediate environment. I looked within my heart and found the thought of doing this was in line with my purpose of impacting lives. This would be one of the vehicles to make that happen.

That was the beginning of my cause called "Live And Not Die" (LAND), which was birthed on 18th August 2017—a platform where we create awareness about mental health and suicide prevention.

This has led to several collaborations I have had with people and organizations across my continent (and beyond!) in order to achieve a mentally healthy society.

I knew this cause was work on its own and I was sold out to doing it. If that must stand, I would have to quit my job. I called my immediate family members and a couple of close friends to hint to them.

"This is risky" was part of my fearful thoughts. "How could you leave paid employment in a nation with an unstable economy to start something you're not sure of?" More questions kept coming. Way back then, the stigma attached to mental health was at its peak. "So, how would you thrive?" was another follow-up question among many others flying through my head.

But you know what, in times such as this, where confusion precedes our clarity, we often look at our hands rather than into our hearts. Do I have enough money? What am I holding on to as per my savings? These are good questions, no doubt, because I do believe in planning as much as you can. But sometimes, answers from the heart put these questions to rest. Because from the heart comes the love and passion for fulfillment. This was how I overcame this decision-making challenge at that defining part of my life. I followed my heart and trusted my gut.

I launched out and started reaching out to people.

Then I discovered what I call the 3 Ps of passion. Your passion:

Paves way for you

Pushes you forward

Pulls resources towards you

I can still remember how I drafted my resignation letter, typed and sent to the management. That was it. The hurdle of doing it was crossed.

To be sincere, it was a rough beginning and, oh, sometimes it's still rough and tough, isn't that life generally? But one of the things that define us is when we find the true meaning of who we are and how to express it. At this juncture, I must stress the need for us to make creating and finding support within our immediate circle of family and friends an important part of our lives. I cannot undermine the support I got—and still get—from my family and friends during and after the shift.

Over four years (and still counting), I've been able to run my own business, form alliances with people and other businesses, find time to further my mental health cause, and also contribute immensely to impacting lives within my community and beyond in different areas.

I've been able to create mental health sensitization across different platforms and in organizations within and outside my country.

Some little things count a lot to me. Going back to my former place of work—not once, but twice—to create a holistic conversation and support surrounding mental wellness for the employees was one of those moments for me. What a way to give back to an organization I had been a part of a couple of years back.

Your own story might not lead you to quitting your job; as a matter of fact, your job might be what you're passionate about, and possibly where you will find fulfillment. The bottom line is you realizing the need to keep releasing yourself to that higher calling, where your fulfillment lies, even if you have to start by doing it afraid. Now that statement has been one of my greatest lessons in life.

Kunle Pelemo, also known as K.P., is a multi-talented nation-building and knowledge business strategist. A down-to-earth and unconventional public speaker, he has been speaking in conferences, seminars, workshops, and events since 2002, when he was in the University. The testimonials and feedback from his clients and attendees are volumes too much for a brief text. He is currently the Lead Strategist of *Mycarebuddy*, an online mental health platform in Nigeria; and Co-founder of Harmony Circle, an Indo-Nigerian collaboration for suicide prevention in Nigeria and India. He is an advocate of mental health and suicide prevention in Nigeria and Africa at large, and also a global goodwill ambassador. Having worked in the oil and gas downstream sector of his country for close to a decade, he deemed it fit to quit the sector in order to champion his mental health and suicide prevention cause called Live And Not Die (LAND).

Connect with Kunle on LinkedIn:

https://www.linkedin.com/in/kunle-pelemo-6201b290

"Keep Going. Your hardest times often lead to the greatest moments of your life. Keep going. Tough situations build strong people in the end."

Roy T. Bennett

Chapter 10
Gail Flowers... Yellow Butterfly

A Yellow butterfly is what I said you'd be when the Good Lord Came to set You free.

You always wore a smile Even when you were in pain

The comfort I feel now is knowing that I will see your smiling face again

Mom you were so Strong and Sweet

My very favorite person on this earth that

I would have the pleasure to meet.

You were always there to lift me up and tell me it was ok

You're going to have your bad days precious but the Lord will lead the way.

Mom I cannot lie it has not been easy here without you

But God has given me the strength to accomplish the things He has planned for me to do So when I see a yellow butterfly I immediately smile and say Thank you, Mom, for the beautiful reminder that you're only a glance away.

Meet Gail Flowers, Founder and CEO of AddVoyces Digital Media Productions. For years, Gail has been supporting small and emerging business owners by offering both professional and affordable digital media productions to help them reach their digital communications and marketing goals.

Gail has a keen knack for selecting just the right elements needed for each individual project with a razor sharp focus on each of her client's unique brands, making a clear distinction between them and their competitors.

Gail's services include video production, podcasts, and voice-overs. She helps her clients produce their digital media content and brings their visions to life.

Gail's website is www.addvoyces.com

"I do not know the details of tomorrow, but I have a hope for a better tomorrows."

Lailah Gifty Akita

Chapter 11

Debra Hult...Not Funny, Not Fair... Where Was God in All of This?

Allow me the opportunity to provide a glimpse into my childhood that caused me to ask, many times, "God, if you loved me, WHY would you allow this to happen?" Life was hard, but I believe that God made me for "hard." The amount of adversity, heartbreak, and disappointment that I came to experience at a young age was certainly not funny and not fair. Resilience and courage are two of my God-given superpowers that I have had an abundance of opportunity to practice. Have I wanted to quit? Heck yes, but by the grace of God go I. I am so grateful for the amazing grace that my Lord had, and continues to have, for me, and for the abundant living I am blessed with today. Regardless of the adversity and challenges along my journey, it is an honor to share a portion of my story.

My parents divorced when I was a month old. Both remarried, and I was then raised by my mom and my stepdad. He was a great man. I considered him my dad because I did not spend any time with my real father. Often, my siblings (I was the youngest of nine) would go to visit him, but mom never allowed me to go. During my very early years, I had a great life; life was good! We were raised on a small farm with goats, chickens, and a huge pig we named after one of my sisters. My mom loved horses, and so do I. I was fortunate enough to have my own horse when I was five years old. I named him "Love," because there was one small white patch in the shape of a heart on his forehead. I was my mom's blue-eyed, white go-go-booted, baton-twirling cowgirl. I was a tomboy at heart, riding my horse, playing in the barn, playing ball, doing the dead man's float in the pool, or collecting salamanders from the brook. On Sundays, I had to put on a dress for church. Most days, my mom cooked oatmeal for breakfast. She would hand me some sugar cubes to give to my horse while I walked to the bus stop. After school, there were the daily chores that come with living on a farm. And, of course, there was homework! I was fortunate that my mom was home when we got off the bus. It made me feel safe and secure. On Fridays before school, my mom would take me to the local diner for breakfast. I was known as the "French Toast Girl" and always felt so special.

However, my world was about to change at the age of seven. It was August. I got off the bus, and mom was not home. She had not been feeling well that morning and went to the doctor. She never came home. She died suddenly from a blot clot that went to her heart; no warning, just gone. She was 36 years old. Six months later, my stepdad, who took us on as his own—and to me was my real dad—bled to death on a factory floor, the victim of a freak accident. He was 37. Not funny, not fair!

My new world was now living with my biological father, a stepmom, and just a few of my siblings. Because my real dad lived 35 minutes away, it meant attending a new school. It didn't take long to understand why my mom had made an effort to prevent me from going to visit my father in the past.

My bedroom was in the uninsulated attic, with sheets that served as dividers to provide some sense of privacy from my other siblings. I can remember lying in my metal army surplus bed at night. I would have my hand covering one ear, while the other ear was listening to music on my alarm clock radio. It was hidden under my pillow so I wouldn't get caught. The music helped to drown out the alcohol-induced fighting and arguing that took place on almost a nightly basis. My heart just ached. I missed what used to be. I was constantly asking myself, "Why, why did my mom and my dad die so young?" There is nothing right and nothing fair about losing your mom and dad when you are seven. When you are seven years old, there are no words that can explain the pain, the loss, the fear, the heartache of wondering why? Why me? What about my birthdays? Who will help me with my schoolwork? What about my graduation? What about my wedding? ...Not funny, not fair!

In the kitchen we had two refrigerators. One had minimal food in it, and the other held a large beer keg with a tap on the door that would get replaced about every two weeks. Hanging on the wall next to that refrigerator was a small wooden doghouse. Next to the doghouse were five wood-carved dogs that represented each of the five siblings. We each had our own dog with our name scribed on it. As soon as you got home from school, you always knew who was in trouble based on whose "dog" was in the doghouse. My stepmother would contrive reasons for us to be in the doghouse. For example, toothpaste would be put on our toothbrush after we left for school so she could tell my dad, when he came home from work, that we didn't brush that morning. Having any time in the bathroom is a challenge when you have that many people in the house and only have one bathroom. Getting hit with the belt in the evenings was almost routine, and it would give my dad a sense of power. My stepmom would lock my dad's snacks and treats in a cabinet so that we did not have access to them. There is no sense behind how mean or dysfunctional a parent can be toward their children, or any child... not funny, not fair.

Even despite all of this, I had that childlike faith that was very dominant. While I blocked my ears at night from the yelling downstairs, there was something deep inside my soul that allowed me to whisper over and over, "I'm going to be something someday. I'm going to be better than all of this and make a difference! I'm going to be on a stage somewhere, somehow, doing something with my life that is significant." My brother Terry, who was six years older, would hear that whisper through the sheets and say back to me, "Say it again Deb... say it again. You got this." Terry was my protector. My father got violent when he drank, and Terry would take the blows from my father that were intended for me, as well as the others. Terry was my rock, my mentor. I had the opportunity to play five years of high school sports, not because I stayed back, but because I started early. I had some natural talent, and I grew into the athlete I became because of the time and patience Terry invested in me. He would often say, "I know you're missing mom. C'mon, let's go throw the ball, you are going to be OK!" Just two weeks after I made the softball team up at the high school as an eighth grader, Terry was suddenly killed. Since then, I have lost three other siblings due to drugs and alcohol as a contributing factor. Not funny, not fair!

Where was God in all of this? How do you maintain any faith at all, or even begin to agree with others when they say things happen for a reason? Yet, I know that it was the Lord who gave me the strength and resiliency to not give up, to not be skeptical, to not have a victim mentality! God used other people in my life to "show up" at the right time and the right season, people who supported and sometimes challenged my mindset, but who always moved me forward to significance.

From the beginning of time there has been good versus evil. As humans, we have the freedom to choose. There are two wars that go on inside of us, good versus evil. Which one will win? It will be the one that you feed. The circumstances that happened in my life were people-driven. It was the people who chose to be evil, not God. God gives us a spirit of love, but we must choose whether to practice that or not. If our identity is based on our pain, then most likely we will choose a spirit of anger, disappointment, frustration, abuse. Hurt people will hurt people.

Despite all my pain, suffering, and turmoil, without a doubt Jesus protected me through it all, though at times it was not funny and certainly not fair. But I survived, and that vision of being on a stage, of being better than my circumstances, of making a difference, is exactly what I get to do today. That pain continues to heal; it is actually what equips me with passion and compassion to be that girl I dreamed and envisioned at ten years old. I get to travel across the country and empower students to be a better version of themselves, to enhance their social and emotional intelligence and their self-worth. By the grace of God, I have been given the gift to empower people—more importantly, empowering them to not allow their wounds to become their identity, and to understand that circumstances do not have to define you. God is bigger than it all.

Deb Hult is co-founder of Core Trainings, an internationally recognized human development company. She is a certified Maxwell Leadership Team Speaker, Coach, and Trainer, as well as a highly sought after national and international Motivational Speaker, Leadership Trainer, and Mindset Coach with an expertise in Relational Leadership. She has been committed to enhancing and empowering students, young women, student athletes, and adults for over 15 years. With her WHY I CAN mindset, Deb is well known for her enthusiastic, positive, and authentic personality, with a speaking style that never gets boring! Deb, despite the many personal challenges and tragedies she has had to overcome, defines the word RESILIENCY. Her realistic approach is courageous and empowering, and it makes a positive difference to all who meet her. She is part of many global initiatives, a recipient of impacting awards, and a partner of many schools, athletic organizations, and corporations. She is humbly honored to always be a part of others' lives and create the difference of positivity.

Deb resides in New Hampshire, USA. Married for 29 years, she is a mother of twin boys who are her world.

www.coretrainings.com

Instagram: @core.trainings

Twitter: @coretrainings

Facebook: Deb Hult

Chapter 12

Rachel Dubin... Finding Grace Through Pain

My name is Rachel Dubin. I am a current student at La Cañada High School. I want to pursue my passion to understand the human mind. I have a great fascination for how our psychological makeup makes humans the way they are. I intend to pair this curiosity with helping others through their traumatic experiences. I want to advocate for teens and young adults who feel they don't have a voice in their experiences and give them a space to share freely. I am interested in plant medicines and hope to discover how we can pair talk-therapy with the use of psychedelics in the future. I believe I can help people heal, not by using pharmaceutical numbing agents, but instead with natural medicines that can break down the walls of post-stress. But most importantly, I want people to know their emotions are a shared experience. My goal in this lifetime is to help souls find grace through their pain.

When I think of a challenging time in my life, my mind immediately turns to an experience where I had absolutely no control over my emotional state. There is no greater challenge than figuring out how to overcome something you don't even understand. When I was ten years old, my world completely changed.

My parents had been struggling in their marriage, and I was overly exposed for some time. Trying to navigate how to provide comfort for both parents was a weight on my shoulders that I did not know did not belong to me. As a child, your parents are your world—they're supposed to be your rock. But what does a child do when they have to be the support system for their parents? Seeing your role models in a crippling state is baffling, and it seemed to me I needed to make it better. I put that responsibility on myself when I had no tools of wisdom. Then, around Christmas of 2016, my dad suddenly died from a heart attack.

Mountains of emotions were overflowing that I didn't even know were possible to feel. My ten-year-old mind simply shut down to a point where I felt nothing. My brain was not developed enough to cope, let alone *comprehend*, such a sickening, life-altering experience. While my young mind tried to navigate how to grieve, the biggest challenge I faced with loss at a premature age was how to *feel* again.

When we think of challenges in our lives, we tend to gravitate towards external experiences. While my external life was dramatically changed, the biggest obstacle I faced was within my own mind. I floated in existence for several years. I did not know what my sadness meant. I did not know what loss or grief was. I did not know that these words had instantly overlapped and been thrust into my life. All I knew was one day my father was here, and just like that, he was gone.

Not knowing my own emotions, I tried to think of the proper reaction to the loss of a parent. Did I cry enough? Did I grieve enough? I felt alone in my experience, while everyone else around me grieving the loss of my father were fully grown adults. They had a community, but where was mine? In an effort to fit in with other fourth graders, I completely blocked out the massive loss I had experienced. I didn't want to make my friends around me uncomfortable, because if I did not know how to deal, they surely had no clue how to be in my presence. As a result, I didn't talk about it. Didn't think about it. And eventually, I didn't *feel* it.

I experienced dissociative episodes as a consequence of shutting off my emotions. A few years after the loss of my father, I struggled to feel emotional responses to daily activities. I didn't feel the highs but—more frighteningly—I never felt the lows. My brain was accustomed to blocking out *any* feeling. I grew frustrated and felt even more broken. I wanted more than anything to feel some sense of normalcy. To my knowledge, I was the only kid at school who had lost a parent, who didn't have a picture perfect family.

The first time I can recall opening up about my traumas was when I was 14. I had just begun a friendship that I still hold to this day. This individual was the first person I had met who didn't have a perfect family.

Now, I want to acknowledge that this was the only person who didn't have a picture perfect family to *my* understanding. Had speaking out about dysfunctional family life been normalized, feelings of loneliness in experience would not have happened.

It provided me immense comfort and relief to discover I was not alone. While our experiences were different, we shared the struggle of trying to navigate through the familial burdens we carried with a premature mind. Slowly, from this point on, I began breaking down walls that had been set in place for years.

Allowing myself to find the point in which I was ready to begin the journey of healing had to come naturally.

It was all still so confusing—people would tell me the "stages" of grief were different for everyone. So, in all honesty, I cannot put a label on where I was in my journey of grief when I started to open up. I can, however, describe the state of mind I was in: too many emotions had built up and were begging to be released from my consciousness.

I had reached a point where I was able to acknowledge what I had gone through. Call it "acceptance," but I don't believe such a subjective process can be defined. I think this creates a pressure to follow a specific path of healing. This only stressed me, and I had to allow myself to organically find me again. I think, in experiencing trauma as a child, time really does help. Having a few more years on this earth allowed me to be able to begin to comprehend everything that had happened to me. I was trying to make sense of the loss of my father and why it made me emotionally "dysfunctional." I struggled to get to the root of an experience greater myself. Once I discovered what this greater meaning was, I was finally able to find grace in the pain.

During the year of the pandemic in 2020, and through the force of being solely my own company, I, like many, began the exploration into who I was. Through inner deep-diving, I began to grasp the awareness of the spiritual experience that is life on earth.

For so many years, I pitied myself. I would ask the universe or God, "Why me?"

The day I changed my mindset, the world around me changed. Switching the way I thought changed the way I acted, changing the way I chose to live my life.

Rather than, "Why did I deserve to endure this pain?" I began to question, "What am I supposed to *learn* from this experience?"

Rewriting the way I viewed life-altering events in my childhood that I felt were out of my control allowed me to find my power. Tragedy is inevitable, but I had a choice if I was going to let it define me. The moment I understood the loss I faced was not random, but rather an opportunity to grow, I found grace, I found hope, I found meaning. Through my spiritual awakening, I turned my helplessness into control. I realized that I was the creator of my own reality, and my thoughts manifest into the physical world around me.

Such a great personal power allowed me to find the strength that comes from pain. I could see for the first time the integrity and resilience that lied within me. My faith in a higher power allowed me to make peace and adapt to external life changes. In order to do so, I had to do the inner work, which is ultimately what allowed me not just to survive, but to thrive.

There are so many lessons I learned through having to grow up quickly due to the instability in my world, starting with this realization:

I cannot prevent the curveballs the universe will throw at me, but I can choose how I move forward with them.

Understanding the greater scheme of my soul's purpose on earth allowed me to make peace with the loss of my father. Knowing my father had his own lessons to learn and his death was not an end, but rather a new beginning, provided immense comfort. It allowed me to make peace with the idea of death itself—seeing it as not something to fear, but something to celebrate.

I turned an indescribable, incomprehensible pain into an opportunity to spiritually grow.

Rachel Dubin

"Love is patient. Love is kind. Love always forgives, trusts, supports, and endures. Love never fails. When every star in the heavens grows cold, and when silence lies once more on the face of the deep, three things will endure: faith, hope, and love."

Jim Butcher

CHAPTER 13

PORTIA BOOKER...
A LEAK IN THIS
OLD BUILDING

When there is a leak, the first instinct is to determine its location to prevent more damage. A leak is a leak. Let's be honest here, an old building already contains many other issues, but an unsealed leak can erode the foundation quicker than Pepsi on an ancient penny. What if a "leak in an old building" has a spiritual message about life and transition (death)? What if the "leak" from an old building (physical body) is fueling the soil for the new building (spirit) that is not created by humans?

My brother's friend Alexander experienced the loss of his older sister. I never knew he had other siblings, but I guess every day is a learning experience. In my own life, I had experienced a loss, too. My own mother had made her transition from earth three months prior. My mind was still working to process and accept the permanence of her no longer being here physically. How could I take on the sadness and range of emotions from another individual while working through my own pain and sorrow? Do I have the emotions to give?

Alexander had been around my family for the past decade. He was present when my great-grandmother made her transition in 2018. Before my own mother's hourglass full of sand ran dry, he came up to the hospital to see her for the last time. I can't forget how much he called my mother "Ma" as well, as she had adopted him as her own. I mean, both my brother and Alexander appeared to be twins separated at birth. Do I need to share the story of how my brother hacked Alexander's Facebook and changed his profile photo to his own? Nobody noticed the difference for six months. But that's for another book.

The night before Alexander's sister's funeral, I heard a message from God: "Portia, please check on Alexander about the arrangements for the service." I was in the middle of cleaning out my closet stacked full of clothes (my own) from prehistoric adulthood. I recognized the day marked exactly three months since my own mother's transition. During the first and second months of my mom no longer being present, I took it very hard. The waterworks show consumed my entire being on those days, and I would apologize to everyone I spoke to about crying with them over the phone. In this third month of my mother reaching her new assignment beyond the physical realm, I placed a strong grip on gratitude. Keeping my focus in this space gave me extra armor to reach out to Alexander.

I sent him a text message to ask how he was doing. He relayed the exact emotions of how I felt during the transition of my own mother: sadness, anger, confusion, hopelessness. His sister transitioned on a sudden basis, whereas my own mother's transition had been a slow progress. I had watched my mother go from using oxygen upon occasion to being fully dependent upon it. Alexander's sister was here one day and gone the very next, without the promise of another exchange or interaction with loved ones. I believe, in my heart, to this day, that this was another reason I reached the finish line called *acceptance* faster than most going through grief.

I felt a tug at my spirit to take action. After residing in this boat called *grief*, I was given an armor called *fortitude*. God covered me with it so I could bring an ounce of joy and hope to others as I went through the process myself. I shared with Alexander the link to my grief series on *Groove with Portia*. In my eyes, this "leak" of compassion I was able to give brought me comfort.

I'm grateful for how transparent my mother was about her final wishes. Ever since I was a teenager, she always told me and my brother to cremate her instead of holding a funeral service. When "liftoff"—or her celebration-of-life day—rolled around, the emotional rollercoaster took me on a mild spin instead of a complete power tower drop. During my mother's balloon release, I recall the outpour of love and support from my family. Alexander released a balloon in honor of her impact on his life. My mother radiated unconditional love. She made everyone family, whether it was a first meeting or second. Nobody wore a stranger hat around her. This "leak" was reciprocated: an earth angel took photos of the balloon release over Lake Erie for me. She told me her own mother who transitioned stopped her and said someone would need these later.

Alexander needed the extra support. He showed up for me and my brother during the transition of my own mother. I wanted to reciprocate. I already had a strong feeling the service would be tough for me. It would resemble a service for my own mother, even though my family did an alternative celebration of life. Before I left the house, I asked God for the right words to encourage someone today. "Please use me to do your will."

Upon arrival at the funeral home, I felt the surge of emotions pull a Mike Tyson uppercut to my gut. I told myself, "Portia, everything is okay. You are safe." I'm glad I remembered to put extra tissue in my pocket in case the waterworks show made its debut. I found a seat a few rows behind Alexander and his family. Several individuals were already crying. On a screen diagonal from the front row was a picture collage with music playing in the background. I noticed the song changed to "Take Me to the King" by Tamela Mann. Immediately, the tears began to fall down my eyes. This was my mother's favorite song. I recalled, before she made her transition in the hospital, that I played this song and she sang along to it before she opted into the morphine drip. I closed my eyes and saw a vision of my mother with a white robe and her beautiful smile. I also noticed a warm touch on my right shoulder. I knew it was my mother letting me know that she is with me always.

The pastor made his way to the front of the funeral home to begin the homegoing service. He began with scripture and then a short song from one of the family members. Due to the amount of people present, the pastor changed the order of the service to allow individuals to share remarks with the family.

One individual came up and sang the song "There's A Leak In This Old Building" by LaShun Pace. I remember my mother playing this song many times in my house. I found myself beginning to sing the song in my head. Hearing it this time struck a chord within my emotional well. The following lyrics bopped me with a revelation:

"There's a leak in this old building, yo and my soul,

Has got to move

I've got another building

A building not made by man's hands."

The leak in an old building was a reminder to me that our spirit is eternal. My mom's old building (body) had a steady "leak" for a long period of time, but each one of us does when we come into the world. The "leak" (hourglass full of sand) is our timeline in our physical body. Little do we know when the hourglass will run out of time, but the leak is slowly building a new "spiritual" foundation for our next assignment in life from this earth. My mom's transition was a reminder for me to pursue my goals and dreams, as we all have a "leak" in our building called life and we never know when the well will run dry.

After the song concluded, I felt a soft nudge on my right leg. It reminded me of when I was a little girl in church who did not know any better about being "ladylike." I enjoyed sitting with my legs wide open in a dress, because in my mind, as a child, what truly was the difference between wearing pants or a dress? I heard the voice of my mom, "Portia, get up! Say something to this family." I did not know what I was going to say, but I trusted in the guidance of my mother and God. I rose from my seat and walked towards the podium. I greeted everyone with both an expression of gratitude and condolence. I allowed my mom to speak through me, to give this grieving family words of hope. Little did I know, each word expelled from my mouth would add an ounce of light into the lives of these individuals. I said a prayer earlier that day for the words to encourage someone today. Thank you God for keeping your promise.

Portia Booker, better known as Portia The Producer, is a Producer, Author, and Multimedia Storyteller from Cleveland, Ohio. She is the host of *Groove with Portia Talk Radio Show and Podcast* which airs every Wednesday on WOVU (95.9 FM) to over 90,000 listeners locally. Portia's show features guests who have turned adverse circumstances in their lives into an opportunity. She is also the host on the *Soulful Conversations Podcast* with Dawn Airhart Witte and Stephanie Young. Portia is the author of "Finding Grace within Grief: Her Transition... My Transformation," a personal narrative on how to see the benefits held within the grief process instead of the societal narrative of holding a heavy deficit. When Portia is away from hosting *Groove with Portia*, she can be found coaching new or veteran podcasters on how to improve their performance, taking photos, listening to audiobooks, visiting museums, hitting the road for a road trip, or walking her furry companion Mr. Fletcher Blaze.

"Faith is unquestioning belief."
Ronald Hopfer

Chapter 14

Nana Kontor Nketiah... An Account of My Faith in God

When Adam Smith theorized that "human needs are insatiable," he was perhaps considering only the physical, socioeconomic, and psychological dimensions of life, without reference to the spiritual dimension, which in actual fact permeates the entire existence of humanity. As a matter of fact, there is a deep yearning in every human being—regardless of creed, race, gender, background, orientation, values systems, or environment—for some transcendent experience, an experience beyond the physical and mundane events and occurrences of life. This is the cradle of my faith in God: a yearning, a search for meaning, purpose, and the expectations of my life. If Adam Smith's theory, which I affirm, ever holds true in any sense, then its claims must be more on the spiritual perspective of human need. For the yearning of every soul for the transcendent is the true mark of humanity.

My name is Nana Kontor Nketiah, and in this brief article, I present an account of my faith in God and what challenges and prospects it has brought to me. My faith and my belief in God are founded on the Bible and my religio-cultural background as an African. As an African, I am notoriously religious. My identity cannot be complete without a description of a religious coloration of every event and activity of my life. Fundamentally, I believe that human beings are a composition of two distinct, but infused, elements: the body (made of dust/clay), which is the physical part, and the spirit (an impartation of life by a sovereign God, whom I describe as the transcendent Being).

The idea of God's sovereignty is the starting point of my faith. Despite this idea being an integral part of my socio-cultural worldview, my personal interpretation of God's greatness, omnipotence, and omnipresence, as well as how he deals with me personally, is what dictates my faith and gives meaning to my life. It defines my allegiance and accounts for the reason I can't go even one day without being in touch with God. Faith is assurance that my life is sacred; it is a gift graciously given to me for which I may be a steward. Faith is the reliance on the giver of life in every situation of life, with the firm conviction that he knows and understands better, and is in a better position to grant me all the necessary resources required to navigate life to its safe ultimate destination.

I grew up in a Christian family. My parents love God, and they introduced me and my siblings to God. Daily morning prayer sessions and weekly attendance and participation in church services were nonnegotiable. Soon, the Bible became the rule for life, even at an early age. However, these were only routines that did not have a lot of meaning until I was old enough. After high school, I began to understand the necessity of having a personal spiritual walk with God. I began cultivating and nurturing my own faith when I came of age.

First, it was out of gratitude to God; then, as the existentialism of life dawned on me and I began assuming roles of responsibility, I realized the need to depend on God and seek his blessings in all things if I were to find success. Thus, my faith in God is borne out of gratitude to God and dependence on his providence and unfailing grace.

I have gratitude because he is my maker, sustainer, and protector. I have been through several transformational phases of life. I have known true hardship and lack. At times, when there appeared to be no hope for the entire family's sustenance, I have learned even from my parents' example that God always makes a way and provides. Therefore, I have always remained grateful for whatever my lot has been.

My dependence upon him stems from the fact that life as a gift from Him can only be truly sustained by Him. I work, I truly work hard. I give my best shot to whatever my hands find to do, but I work with the understanding that it is the blessings of God that makes a person truly worthy. Thus, my faith in God does not operate in a vacuum, but is premised upon the employment of my God-endowed strength, health, talents, abilities, and resources to work to become better. My dependence on God is birthed from my experience that God never fails. He works in very mysterious ways to provide all my needs according to his riches in glory through Jesus Christ, my savior.

I have been through some of the most unimaginable hardships any young man could possibly experience. My crucibles have taught me that the path to the pinnacle is always through the pit, and faith is what sustains a person throughout the journey to the top. The crucible experience is meant to make me fit for the life at the top, and without faith I cannot survive at the top. Sometimes my faith is frustrated, challenged, and rendered illogical. But because I have been intentional and conscious at nurturing it, even when I feel like letting go, I remember how far I have come by faith, and I am encouraged to press forward in hope. When prayers are unanswered and circumstances only grow worse, when plans don't go as intended and every sacrifice begins to fall apart, when you see all your labor getting out of hand into a loss, then faith is our ability to retain resilience and positive composure in the face of such experiences. Faith is our capacity to foresee a tomorrow where green pastures and bright skies will replace the current scarcity and gloomy outlook. Actually, it was during my crucible days that my faith grew stronger and more intimate with God.

My faith has been, and continues to be, nurtured by my engagement in spiritual disciplines such as studying of the Bible, praying, fasting, and—especially—giving. Daily, I present myself, my family and friends, my work, and everything that concerns me, to God in prayer. I do so with the knowledge that everything left in God's hands is left in safe and in abled care. Then I go out to face the day with zeal and a positive mindset. I am sure to return fulfilled and content with whatever gains or losses I make. Actually, faith doesn't mean that things will always go well. Sometimes the worst happens, but I have learned to trust God's sovereignty and wisdom in all situations.

I intend to continue to grow in faith by continually seeking ways to live my faith and to demonstrate it to the people I encounter every day. I do not ever envisage a day or time when I will lose my faith in God, because He has been too good to me, and I know that my future has better prospects with him than in any other system of belief. Thus, my faith is a part and parcel of my very life, and my need for spiritual growth will continue to be insatiable, because the more I learn about God, the more I pray, and the more I seek him, the more I truly need him also.

Keep faith and never give up, because giving up has never been an option in life.

Nana Kontor Nketiah

Nana Kontor Nketiah was a professional banker with over 15 years banking experience. Nana has been actively involved in community services by volunteering with a number of NGOs, such as Foundation For The Mentally Challenged, Rescue Me Foundation International, You At Heart Foundation, Teach for Growth, Impact Sierra Leone, and Desire To Inspire Foundation. He is passionate about helping the poor and needy.

Six years ago, he gave up banking to become a full-time charity worker with The Desire To Inspire Foundation, where he is the Global Development Director. His office has touched and transformed numerous lives through partnerships with other charity organizations.

Currently, he is working on projects that aim to empower the youth through skills training and medical outreach. He also serves as a board member for other similar charities, where he implemented a number of initiatives to enhance skills among the poor and needy in selected communities.

Using his finance and banking experience, he serves as an advisor to the organization he works with. Nana loves driving and listening to music at leisure. Lastly, he believes in learning daily to improve his practice and also to be a change agent wherever he finds himself. He is a native of Ghana, but his works cut across the African continent.

"Life is full of happiness and tears, be strong and have faith."

Kareena Kapoor Khan

Chapter 15

Larita Rice Barnes... Prospering In A Pandemic

^{Isaiah 43: 19} *Behold, I will do a new thing; now it shall spring forth; shall ye not know it? I will even make a way in the wilderness, and rivers in the desert.*

According to the Centers for Disease Control and Prevention (CDC), on March 11, 2020, the Novel Coronavirus Disease (also known as COVID-19) was declared a pandemic by the World Health Organization (WHO). This declaration left many scrambling and worried about what this could mean for their present and their future.

Big businesses that had once dominated the market were now not able to operate as before. Churches, Mosques, Temples, Cathedrals—no matter the size of the building or the congregation—were all forced to shut their doors. Business as usual was suddenly becoming a thing of the past. The hustling and bustling of daily traffic had ceased. Restaurants and pubs were empty inside, and grocery store shelves were almost bare.

Though the pandemic put a halt to many things that we love such as family gatherings, community outings, and traveling across the US and abroad, it helped many of us get some of the needed (albeit forced) self-care that we had refused to take previously, due to the demands of life, business, ministry, family duties, and society. Societal norms say that if you're not busy, you're not banking. In other words, no matter how much wear and tear you may be putting on yourself, dominant culture insists we must be found doing and working—well, grinding may be a better description for some. Grinding says I can't stop, no matter what; even if it's not producing great results, I must keep going. COVID-19 changed all of this. It was like the world stood still, and everyone that lived it stood still with it. There was a quietness upon the earth, yet the sound was so loud. How could this be? I believe it was because the Lord, the Sovereign One, the Most-High, was speaking. Our souls were forced to listen from within. Our hearing was no longer being drowned out by the noise of the world, but rather guided by the Holy Spirit. We were forced to see ourselves for who and what we had become. The good, the bad, and the ugly.

It was almost like a divine encounter: one that called for a supernatural reset, a time of reflection and introspection, a willingness to perhaps shift from what we had once known and become so accustomed. If nothing else, the world knew that we were experiencing something different than this generation had seen before. Something new was unfolding. New norms were being established, like it or not. And it was clear that if we were to progress, we were going to have to pivot.

These are unprecedented times. Never, ever had the world experienced the effects of this particular deadly disease before now. Many struggled to pivot. To this very day, many are still grappling to make sense of what is going on. The impending thoughts on whether things will revert to the way they were seems to almost dominate the day—for some, that is.

The pandemic has revealed the disparities that many face on a day-to-day basis. It also revealed the broken and oppressive systems that were only serving like a turning wheel for hamsters to run. Individuals most affected had motion but no progress. Systems that had not been designed for all to succeed and have a fair share were fully illuminated. And the voices of new warriors began to rise and speak out for justice and righteousness. Though the streets were not being flooded with peaceful protests, social media and newfound ways to use technology began to explode. And the reach to all four corners was greater than it had ever been before.

Right in the midst of a global pandemic, God's word STILL remains true. He said "I use the foolish to confound the wise." In the same breath, I say what we once knew, we will never, ever know again. Old things have passed away, and now we are beholding the new. For some, this is scary and unfathomable, and the grave disruption that has seemingly resulted from this thing called COVID-19 has left an imprint that will go down in history. Generations to come will still be wrestling to forge paths through its rocky terrain.

But we must remain encouraged. There's a quote that says, "Where there's no struggle, there can be no progress." Trials and tribulations come to make us stronger. The Bible says in St. John 12:24 (NIV), "Very truly I tell you, unless a kernel of wheat falls to the ground and dies, it remains only a single seed. But if it dies, it produces many seeds." There are many seeds of newness sprouting up all over the world. Seeds of creativity, innovation, and wittiness are showing their fruits very brightly. Right when some things seem to be shutting down and closing up, many people of God have found themselves in one of the most abundant times of their lives. They are supernaturally eradicating debt, expanding businesses, and literally "Prospering in a Pandemic." The word of God is being manifested. He says "I will make even a way in the wilderness and rivers in the desert."

I went to a conference recently in St. Louis, Missouri. There was a national gospel recording singer by the name of Tye Tribett ministering. He released these words in the atmosphere, he said that sometimes, the way God declares a new thing is to pronounce something dead. This resonated deeply with me, in part because I was seeking God intently on next steps and direction for our ministry. Additionally, I was struggling to give birth to this chapter. I didn't want to just write any old thing. Instead, I wanted it to be fresh, new, revelatory, and from the heart of God. My desire was that as these words are read, someone's life would be revolutionized. I could sense deeply that something major was unfolding and that there was obviously a special anointing upon this project. The opposition to complete this assignment was intense, but the desire to get it done was greater.

I don't know who this word is for, but it's time to pivot. Don't stay stuck. When the Grace is Lifted it's time to be Shifted. One of the greatest lessons that I have learned is to never be completely married to a particular way of doing a thing, but rather, remain open and ready to shift at all times. I was reminded that change doesn't mean that something is wrong, nor does relinquishing the old mean that something is bad. It just means that embracing the new is now necessary: a new way of thinking, a new way of doing, and a new way of just being. For many of us, it means new relationships, new seasons, and new levels. It could mean relocating to a new region or starting a new job or career. However, we can remain confident in knowing that sometimes a path changes direction to fulfill the purpose God has for our lives. Rest assured we are not alone; the giver of all life is with us. God is NOT just the journey; he is also the destination. Come what may. The strongest crops grow best in dung. We will prosper where we are planted. We will not be delayed or denied our inheritance or our rightful place.

Larita Rice-Barnes- Global Political Advisor / CEO & Founder of Global Impact Leadership Alliance™ / Lead Organizer & Founder of RESET America RESET Africa®

Founder of My Pink Stilettos™, Larita is a trailblazer. Innovation, creativity, and networking are her strong gifts. She creates platforms for dignitaries, stakeholders, and everyday citizens to engage in conversations to build shared power for the collective good of those who are marginalized. Larita's work spans across five continents: Africa, Asia, North America, South America, and Europe.

She is an ordained pastor and international chaplain, and she is a transformational leader who has given herself to the work of ministry. She is the founder of Empowerment of Grace. She oversees two churches: Empowerment of Grace-USA and Empowerment of Grace-Uganda. They have outreach ministry extensions in Kenya and India. These outreach ministries focus on serving the poor, sick, and shut-in throughout their local villages. She is also a philanthropist; she supports orphaned children by enabling them to go to school, and she assists widows by supporting efforts for them to become economically stable.

Larita has been awarded for her humanitarian efforts by receiving the President Barack Obama Lifetime Achievement Award in 2017 and the President Joseph R. Biden Lifetime Achievement Award in 2021. She received an Honorary Doctorate in Humanitarianism from the Global International Alliance. She was appointed as Chaplain of the Saint Louis, Missouri–East Saint Louis, Illinois region for Global International Alliance. She is a leader for the USA Ladies of All Nations International (LOANI), representing over 180 countries.

www.globalimpactnow.org

www.resetyourlife2.com

www.mypinkstilettos.com

Facebook- Larita Rice-Barnes

Instagram @laritarocksrice

"Without faith, nothing is possible. With it, nothing is impossible."

Mary McLeod Bethune

CHAPTER 16

LUZ SANCHEZ... DO YOUR BEST, THE REST LEAVE TO GOD

One of the hardest seasons in my life was having my identity stolen. I was tested! Many of us are tested from our mother's womb and throughout the years, over and over. We've come to terms with the fact that our only option is to live our lives as a testament to our faith.

Challenges and obstacles are our training grounds to strengthen our character, attitude, and values. However, some battles are ruthlessly exhausting, and in the middle of them, we don't know how we are going to make it. We do our best, and the rest we leave to God.

I didn't know how I was going to make it. One year before the pandemic, I had two jobs, but I lost the one that was providing me with most of my income. Someone broke into my car and stole my purse and important documents within the same week. I called right away to cancel my debit and credit cards and try to replace the most important documents. I thought that was the end of it.

A month later, a good Samaritan living at one of my old addresses contacted me with tons of mail. I was perplexed and thankful she didn't send the letters back. At twilight, I opened the letters, some addressed to my name, and others to a variation of my name. Some were applications for credit cards to stores, others were purchases for thousands of dollars and rentals I hadn't made; they had even bought two vehicles, an RV and a motorcycle! I didn't even know I had that kind of credit! My head was exploding. I took a moment to hold myself together and closed my eyes, trying to connect to God, trying to figure out what to do. I didn't know where to start. I've always been conscious about the health of my finances.

The letters continued coming—rejected loan applications for huge amounts of money and other purchases. Instead of looking for a job, I had to resolve this! How could I sleep at night knowing someone was getting me into debt as the days went by? How could I sleep knowing someone out there was committing crimes with my identity?

Of course, I went to the police right away. Even for them, it was complex to understand. I persisted with the police until they listened. A detective said to me, "The chances of finding the thief are slim. They are like ghosts. And besides, we are way too busy with so many cases. But, I can tell you where to start." I only needed a ray of hope. One of my mantras is, "I'll do whatever it takes." This mantra is applied to whatever I set my mind to do. My mission this time was to get to the root of this issue until I cleared my name.

Almost three months went by. I had lost my sleep. I had depleted all of my savings, my health was deteriorating, and as a single mom, my heart was aching. I kept on praying every day. From nine to five I would make phone calls, the hours I spent on hold were adding up, day-by-day. I had to send proof to many companies that these charges hadn't been made by me. I did absolutely everything I was asked to do. I made copies of all the letters and sent huge packages to the major credit bureaus. I went in person to the places the vehicles were bought to see if there was something they could do about it after they had sold those vehicles to a thief. I asked for all the details; I asked if they had cameras and anything that could help me to dig deeper. I reported it to several police departments, providing as much information as I could. I journaled literally everything, as much as time allowed. It felt like I was fighting an invisible, giant organized crime organization, and I was just a step behind the criminals.

In the third month, I was utterly exhausted; the situation was suffocating me. Spiritually, something was happening. On random nights, in my slumber, I saw lights flowing inside my room. One of those days, I also saved an ill racoon from spinning in the middle of traffic while picking up my daughter from school. As a nature lover, I thanked God for giving me the opportunity to save the life of this living creature, but the event felt strange to me. Numbers were visible on clocks, car plates, or receipts. Waking up exactly at 11:11, dreaming of 333, 555, and 888. The signs were there, even though they were not visible in the physical realm. I kept it to myself.

Synthetic identity theft was such a painful experience. Throughout my journey to fix this, there were messages that kept me going. A lady at the DMV said to me, "Stay strong. If God is with you, who can be against you?" A quote I read, by Hannah Anderson, impacted me: "Nothing less than God will satisfy you. Nothing less will sustain you. Nothing less will suffice." And my sister in Mexico prayed with me and for me, touched my heart, and gave me strength, saying, "Luz, no one can steal the identity and authority God gave only to you."

It was getting dark, it was twilight; I received a phone call from a police officer, relaying a message that a news station wanted to talk to me. He asked if I had seen the news hours earlier. I told him I don't watch the news. The police had caught a thief in a reckless RV pursuit, with one dog jumping out of the window. There were two in the vehicle. Unfortunately, the driver crashed several times, injuring multiple people and the two dogs, and endangering so many more throughout the chase. She was exposed nationwide.

Several news outlets interviewed me. I had to speak up to warn others to guard their identity. You may think that everything ended there. It didn't. Investigations took time, replacing all my documents took time, and I had to clear things up with insurance and prove that I was not responsible for those vehicles—one having been used as a weapon of destruction. Each and every damage and mess this lady caused took a lot of irreplaceable time, money, and energy.

I know in my heart that God is always watching over me. After friends found out through the news, I received support from my church, through prayers, and from encouraging messages through social media. A lawyer from my congregation took over my case and represented me. There were still so many companies I had to reach out to. After my lawyer took over, a huge weight was lifted off my shoulders. When I talked to the FBI agents and gave them all the evidence, they mentioned that they had recovered important documents from many people inside the RV. According to her police records, she had been on the path of crime and destruction for a long time. If I hadn't gone to lengths I went to and put all my energy into clearing my name, this lady would still be committing all kinds of crimes, harming more human beings.

I've always believed there are blessings in disguise. In the middle of adversity, sometimes it's hard to see the purpose of it. However, the lessons that remain with you strengthen your resilience. Whatever mission you are entrusted by life, you put on your armor and go on the quest to resolve it, no matter the sacrifice. We are light-bearers, messengers of justice, peace, and love. If not you, then who?! If not now, then when? We know there is no time to lose. It is the energy of your faith that says "yes" when others say "no." It is your faith that restores balance and resolution when someone says that chances are slim. Because of faith, suddenly the winds may blow in our favor, and we can feel the hand of God at work.

Keep working on your goals and dreams relentlessly! There may be things that derail you from your purpose, but that does not mean you cannot continue walking on the path with your feet firmly planted on the earth. You must believe it, seeing it in your mind's eye. There are obstacles, but you are a warrior, an overcomer, and a victor. There are circumstances out of your control, but you focus on the things you can work with and bend like a palm tree in the wind. You do your best, say your prayers, and the rest you leave to God.

Luz Sanchez is a filmmaker, author, speaker, and generational breaker. She is from Mexico City, living in Los Angeles, CA.

She graduated with a BA in Cinema and TV Arts. She is a DTM (Distinguished Toastmaster). Luz collaborated on two books, "Life Boosts" and *Women Who Rock 2*. She is an author of the e-book *Stolen Identity - What to do when it happens to you*. She is also a former Ms. Elite Mexico-America at Woman of Achievement Pageant.

SOCIAL MEDIA HANDLES

IG: Luz Sanchez

FB: Luz Sanchez

LinkedIn: Luz Sanchez

Website: luz-sanchez.com

"My faith didn't remove the pain, but it got me through the pain. Trusting God didn't diminish or vanquish the anguish, but it enabled me to endure it."

Robert Rogers

Chapter 17

Doneza Inez Smith... I Believe in You

Doneza Smith was known in her family for always having a vivid imagination, and, having been gifted with a rare vocal ability, she always had big dreams of becoming a large-scale entertainment brand.

Doneza's father was a musician who taught himself how to play all kinds of musical instruments on his own. What he didn't know was that his first born daughter would also be gifted with the talent of music. He started to take time to teach her some basics of music, because he had seen her interest in it and noticed that she might be as gifted in music as he was.

Doneza grew up loving to help people, and she always believed that whatever she put her mind to would pan out. She was determined to become a mover and shaker in the entertainment world, so she started out as an artist manager. She managed various artists from Philadelphia and had a wonderful experience learning the business, despite most of the artists not being prepared to develop their craft and grow into a success story. Little did she know, she was being prepared to meet that one artist who would bring out the best in her.

Doneza worked for a record label called 215 MoneyTeam, which was well known in Philly, and this added more credence to her pursuit of being one of the top music executives in the area. Doneza enjoyed artist management, but she wanted to go deeper into the music entertainment business. She was introduced to a musician and producer, and together they started a label, but she soon learned she was only a ceremonial partner in the label, with nothing to guarantee for her input. Despite being the brain behind the label, she wasn't appreciated for all her efforts. They didn't believe in her, even though she had believed in them.

Doneza knew something was missing from her life. She felt as if she wasn't fulfilling her dreams, and she believed one day she would become a label owner, too, with the right team around her fulfilling that dream: the dream of becoming a music executive, managing one of the biggest brands in the world. She didn't know how this would happen, but she kept on believing.

Doneza teamed up with a movie producer from Atlanta and was introduced to a team of wonderful people, but that wasn't where her heart was. She knew her dreams were still in the music entertainment business, so she held on to her dream and continued on her journey with nothing but hope. She kept on believing until she was at the end of her rope. With all hopes faded, she started to question herself, wondering what on earth she was going to do with all the experiences in the entertainment world she gathered over the years. It all seemed like a waste of precious time, and she was beginning to regret her life.

Doneza prayed to Jehovah and asked him to direct her steps. She looked back at the business plan and said to herself, "You need to rewrite your plans for a new vision and execute it. No more excuses."

Doneza looked into the mirror of her life, and that day she believed in herself again. Suddenly, she had a new slate to work with and to work on.

Meanwhile, in a distant land—the ancient city of Benin in Nigeria, West Africa— a talented artist was also on the verge of giving up, due to the fact that there was no one to help him reach his maximum potential. That artist's name was Nnamdi Ogbonna, also known then as "One," but on instagram he had uploaded a video as *@oneblackjew*. The video was a submission for a song contest.

Somehow, that video popped out of nowhere while Doneza was just scrolling through Instagram. She had been listening to unsigned artists, commenting on their music and just enjoying the music vibes.

Doneza was intrigued by the talent of *@oneblackjew* after watching his song submission for the cover of "Katalambano." She said to herself, "Where is this artist from?" She didn't know he was Nigerian, but it didn't matter where he was located. His sound, ambition, drive, and hunger could be seen and felt.

Doneza reached out on his Instagram page and commented, saying she wanted to hear more music from this man, also known as NewJew. She went down his page to see what else he had posted, and to her amazement, she saw more videos and was impressed.

NewJew commented back to Doneza. He thanked her for liking his videos, and they had a conversation. Eventually, NewJew asked Doneza, "Can I trust you with my music?" and the response he received became the blueprint for how the label Done Deal International was born. He emailed her some of his unmastered music, and when Doneza asked if he was signed to a record label, she was surprised when he said no. He said to her, "Hey, why don't you manage me?" Doneza was shocked. She said, "*What?* Of course! It would be an honor to manage you."

Doneza's life and career path were both changed in that instant. She thanked Jehovah for answering her prayers. That was how she became President of Done Deal International, and Nnamdi Ogbonna became Vice President. Together, they have become one of the fastest-growing record labels on the international scene. NewJew, who now goes by the brand ONEOFAFRICA, went from being an ordinary local boy from Benin City to an internationally recognized name.

ONEOFAFRICA was out there believing one day, his voice would be heard across the world. When Doneza spoke to ONEOFAFRICA, he sounded as if he was on the verge of giving up on his hopes of becoming an inspiring musical artist.

ONEOFAFRICA needed someone out there to believe in him for his dreams to be activated. Then, Doneza came into the picture, already prepared to believe in him. The Dream Mission, started by Doneza and ONEOFAFRICA, became the first breakthrough for both of them. ONEOFAFRICA's Dream Mission is a non-profit that caters to the untapped creative potentials in Africa.

This breakthrough was made possible because Doneza believed and ONEOFAFRICA believed, and the power of belief has raised their combined potential into the limelight.

She believed that his voice was marketable and she knew that she would be able to take his music from the local scene to an international stage. And he believed in her, knowing she was destined to be his international brand manager and business partner, and that together, they would move and shape the world as Done Deal International LLC. ONEOFAFRICA just needed someone to believe in him, and Doneza needed a teammate to help her build an entertainment empire that is set to last for generations.

Done Deal International's vision is to achieve global recognition for their relevance in the growth, development, and sustainability of businesses across the world.

Done Deal International's mission is to collaborate with businesses globally from diverse sectors for growth development and sustainability.

Doneza manages The ONEOFAFRICA Dream Mission, The ONEOFAFRICA Believe Mission, and also Chaiboboponsession, the comedy brand of ONEOFAFRICA.

Doneza has booked shows for ONEOFAFRICA in the United States, even throughout the trying times of the pandemic. They have a lot of great things happening behind the scenes, with more to come. They can be found on social media at @donedealinternational   @oneofafrica   @chaiboboponsession https://www.donedealinternational.com

https://www.oneofafrica

Doneza's affirmation is to never stop believing in yourself. No matter what happens, keep going and never give up!

Doneza would like to thank Ms. Dawn Airhart Witte for this wonderful opportunity and the experience to share with the world the story of Done Deal International. Thank you also to ONEOFAFRICA and Done Deal International LLC.

Doneza Inez Smith was born in Philadelphia, PA, to Susan Smith and the late Quincy Lee Thomas, Sr. Doneza grew up in South Philadelphia. She was raised by her mother in a single family home. Doneza's father Quincy was into music—he was a band member, composer, and singer; in her early days, she remembers dancing to the music played in both homes as she grew up.

Doneza's passion for music grew as time went on. She remembers her father saying, "When you grow up, you will have a voice." And later, she did. Doneza went to Bok Vocational Technical School, where she took up cosmetology. That was her passion, she could do any style and cut any hair texture.

After graduating high school in 1994, Doneza worked at hair salons, but she found out later that she could make more money doing hair at home, so she did that. Doneza has two children, Canoesha and Jovell Nelson, who watched her while she hustled to make ends meet. Canoesha, Doneza's eldest child, was born with cerebral palsy, but she never let anything stop her from tending to her children; she was determined to keep pushing, no matter how difficult things had gotten. She had the support of her mother, Susan, and step-father, Paul Smith.

As Doneza continued on to find her way through life, she was able to get her family into a brand new accessible home that would help her daughter with her disability. Doneza went on to become a home health aide, because she was very caring and always had a heart for helping those with disabilities.

Doneza's passion for music was still there, even though life presented some challenges. She stumbled upon an app called "Smule Sing" and met wonderful artists much like herself; she fell in love with singing again.

Doneza always had a bigger plan. She teamed up with a friend who had a music company, but came upon some setbacks. Doneza again knew that she wanted more, so when she met an artist along her journey by the name ONEOFAFRICA, she and he spoke about what their dreams were, and the two decided to take a leap of faith and go into business together. They created Done Deal International, LLC. To date, the company is doing great. Doneza manages international artist ONEOFAFRICA; she took his music from being a name solely recognized in Nigeria to being an internationally-recognized brand across the globe.

"Faith is taking the first step even when you don't see the whole staircase."

Martin Luther King, Jr.

Chapter 18

Valerie C. Thompson... Believe- The Word

Believe – The Word

Let us start with the word *believe*. This word is defined as "to accept something as true, to have a firm conviction of the ability to do something." It also means to trust and accept there is something majestic about you and me! Now, let us break down the word *believe* into three syllables: be-lie-ve. These three words are powerful, and power-filled.

Be translates into "exists, live, have life, breathe, take place, and come to pass." Those words speak to the very reason we are here today! *Lie* means "to keep resting in a horizontal position; to remain in a specified state." It also means "to state something that is not true." When we experience something in life, we usually say, "I do not like what happened to me," when in fact, we should be changing our words to "That did not happen *to* me, it happened *for* me." This allows us to let go of the lie that came to kill, steal, and destroy our livelihood.

Ve is defined as "have." We have seen this attached to many words such as "we've," meaning "we have." Therefore, if we take *ve*, which really means *have*, and break that down, have is defined as "possess, own, occupy, experience, enjoy, taste" and this excites me! How about you? Let us take a closer look at what these three words mean when we combine them to create the weighty word **BELIEVE**!

In the beginning, God called us into existence to have life, to experience life, to multiply, and to live abundantly on every level! God breathed life into us, and we came to existence. Therefore, we were already in a vertical state, *upright*. While living life, we have all experienced trials and tribulations which have come in the form of abuse, poverty, disease (creating dis-ease), drug addiction, alcoholism, and mental illness. These are better known as *lies*, which have knocked us down, causing us to lie down in a horizontal position mentally, physically, spiritually, and financially! These lies have separated us from our creator, family, friends, and purpose.

Therefore, it is our duty, while here on Earth for a limited time only, to get up and take what is rightfully ours mentally, physically, spiritually, and financially. As mentioned earlier, the lies come to kill, steal, and destroy our thoughts of who we really are. We are predestined; therefore, God already knew about our greatness! God already knew we could stand the test of time because we are built to last! God already knew what our assignment, aka purpose, would be!

Once we remember who we are, it is our duty to have to have life, to have peace, to have a mindset that will propel us to our best lives so we can live our purpose! We are created to dismantle systems, patterns, and cycles, so our relationships can be restored so we can soar! Unfortunately, we live in a society where lies keep us asleep, lying horizontally, therefore we are not encouraged to do the internal healing work. We continue to downplay who and what we are and operate from a place of pity and not power.

My name is Valerie C. Thompson. The "C" stands for courage! I am created to encourage, inspire, uplift, and empower the masses. It is time to dismantle the lies! It is time to own your truth and RISE! It is time to stop saying "hurt people hurt people!" It is time to believe healed people heal people! It is time to let go of the childhood trauma, adult drama, and live life on purpose for God's huge purpose! I hope you are blessed by my heart share.

"Valerie, I know you are in there!" shouted my husband. My heart felt like it leaped out of my chest as I looked through the peephole of Motel 6 and saw my husband's eye piercing through the peephole on the opposite side of the door. Several days later, my husband was helping me move my belongings out of storage and back to our home. Needless to say, this started a cycle of me leaving and returning, a spiral of domestic violence, a relationship with a narcissist. Well, this was not the beginning. This cycle started long ago when I was in my mother's womb.

The Womb and the Lies!

The womb is the birthing ground for all creation, both physical and spiritual. When a child is conceived, the enemy comes in like a thief in the night, to kill, steal, destroy, and plant lies. The enemy (inner-me) of doubt, fear, hate, shame, guilt, low-self value, division, pride, toxicity. Did my mother speak life to me while I was in her womb? Did her mother bless her with affirmations while she was in the womb? My Spirit tells me my mother and grandmother did not identify with the importance of nurturing the womb. Not their fault, they could only give away what they had in their glass. Did they believe in a different way, a better way? The function of the womb is to nourish and house a fertilized egg until the fetus is ready to be delivered.

How about my great-grandmother? What was her experience? I'll tell you what, if I keep going down my family tree, I will eventually run into my great, great, great grandmother who was snatched from her mother's arms, raped repeatedly, sold, and beaten in chattel slavery. You might say, "What does this have to do with anything?" I say, it has a lot to do with everything!

You see, if healing does not take place in the family system, cycle, lineage, history will repeat itself. Have you ever been around someone who said, "I do it because my mother did it." Well, that does not make it right. Imagine being raped only to find out you are pregnant. Imagine, while you are carrying the baby of someone who has taken your innocence away, how the fear, frustration, anger, depression, suicidal thoughts, anxiety, and pain are compounded daily.

Every emotion a mother feels is passed down to the child. When one is riddled with oppression, depression, and abuse daily, there is minimal chance that love and affection is rendered to the unborn child. It is likely this child will reflect the environment of the caretaker. This is known as generational trauma—the psychological effects of trauma have been transferred from one generation to the next.

The function of the womb is to nourish and house a fertilized egg until the fetus is ready to be delivered. If the mother does not believe, how can the child believe? My mother was in a domestic violence relationship with my father. Her parents, my grandparents, were in a domestic violence relationship. In every generation, history was repeated based on what they knew. No one ever told them their temporary situation could change if they believed it could.

Faith!

I believe I was created for something greater than merely reliving my childhood, which was riddled with observation and absorption of domestic violence. I believe I do not want my children to repeat history with restraints and constraints in their mindset. One of my favorite scriptures is Hebrews 11:1 (paraphrased), *Faith is being sure of what you hope for and certain of what you do not see.* In those early days, I had to see in the spiritual realm (imagination) what I did not see in the physical realm.

Walking by faith, also known as imagining a better life for myself, husband, children, and grandchildren, led me on a journey of self-discovery and inner healing. Everything we desire starts with a thought first. It starts in the mind, in a dark place. The creation of a manifestation begins with the thoughts we believe for ourselves. In comparison, it is no different than if one believes the world was formed through a thought from God in the stillness of darkness. Hebrews 11:3 states, [By] *faith we understand that the universe was formed at God's command, so that what is seen was not made out of what was visible.* Read that again and be inspired!

Action!

I began to pray from a place of desired state rather than a place of "lack." As an example, "I wish, or I want" rather than "I am, and thank you, God." You see, it is up to us to create the lifestyle we desire. We must implement THANKFULNESS, DISCIPLINE, FOCUS, DETERMINATION, AND PERSEVERANCE daily without making excuses. We must make bold moves and take small steps out of our familiar zone daily! You have heard people say, "Step out of the box," I say *create the box*! Imagination and creativity are keys to unlock our greatest potential!

Walk in courage! Dream big! Get comfortable with the unknown and allow God to blow your mind! I sat on the edge of my couch in 2020 and gave birth to Own Your Truth & Rise! We are fearfully and wonderfully made! When we believe the truth and demolish the lies, we live and RISE!

Life does not always paint a picture clear enough for one to understand.

Valerie Thompson was created to encourage, inspire, and to uplift women, one at a time.

Valerie C. Thompsonm also known as "Valerie-The-In-Courage-Her," has a heart for women who have experienced childhood trauma from the shackles of domestic violence.

Unresolved childhood trauma turns into adult drama if healing does not take place.

Valerie is the founder of Own Your Truth & Rise Coaching/Consulting, wherein she provides clients with the support needed to take ownership of their healing, and to provide them with various strategies, so that they can operate *in purpose, on purpose, for God's huge purpose!* Valerie helps her clients to recognize their temporary circumstance as a catalyst for the creation of a new life.

Valerie is the visionary of The Woman The Gifts; (hosted virtually as the Spirit leads to empower women), host of a podcast titled *Own Your Truth and Rise*, and writer for the virtual magazine, *Santana Global Magazine!*

Valerie is also the author of e-book, Your *Soul is Free – Encouragement from A to Z*, Co-author of *Before the Vows Break: Tales of Triumph*, co-author of best-selling book *Finally Free*, co-author of *Women Who Pray* and co-author for best sellers *Reinvented to Rise* and *Fierce, Fabulous, and Free!* Most recently, the visionary over *From Trauma & Drama to Truth!*

Valerie is a mother of four gifted and talented children and a grandmother of phenomenal twins!

Valerie C. Thompson – I AM because God is the great, I AM!

"Faith consists in believing when it is beyond the power of reason to believe."

Voltaire

Conclusion

I am beyond blessed to have such inspiring and supportive people in my life, and it is an honor to be able to share their voices with you. Every story in this book has given me such hope and inspiration. Each chapter has reinforced all that I believe about the world we live in and our place in it.

I was not going to write a conclusion, but something happened this morning that felt like another nod from the Universe or a wink from God that this book was meant to be. I have known a music artist named ONEOFAFRICA from Nigeria for a few years through social media. He is a very talented musician, and one of his dreams is to have his music reach beyond the continent of Africa. I love being able to help people make their dreams come true, so the thought came to me to ask him if he would like to perform at our virtual book launch. I sent him a photo of our cover and his response was, "Wow, and I have been talking about the power of believe for the past two years now."

My entire body became electrified. He then sent me a photo of his book called "Believe Mission." Seeing that cover and reading what he wrote moved me to tears, because when my title, *Believe*, came to me all of those years ago, I would not have imagined how powerful this book would be. God gives us signs all of the time to let us know we are on the right path. When we lean into the Divine, our dreams will turn out even better than we can imagine. Every aspect of this book is proof.

I hope this book and all of the wisdom contained within has given you faith, hope, and love. I know that is what it has done for me. Look for future editions to be released soon, because there are so many more stories to share about the power of faith, hope, and love. The magic that happens when we "BELIEVE…"

Ubuntu,

Dawn

"Faith is not the belief that God will do what you want. It is the belief that God will do what is right."

Max Lucado

"And above all, watch with glittering eyes the whole world around you because the greatest secrets are always hidden in the most unlikely places. Those who don't believe in magic will never find it."

Roald Dahl

"There is never a moment when God is not in control. Relax! He's got you covered."

Mandy Hale

"Faith is a knowledge within the heart, beyond the reach of proof."

Kahlil Gibran

"The function of prayer is not to influence God; but rather to change the nature of the one who prays."

Soren Kierkegaard

"We have always held to the hope, the belief, the conviction that there is a better life, a better world, beyond the horizon."

Franklin D. Roosevelt

"Hope is important because it can make the present moment less difficult to bear. If we believe that tomorrow will be better, we can bear a hardship today."

Thich Nhat Hanh

"Hope is a waking dream."

Aristotle

www.ingramcontent.com/pod-product-compliance
Lightning Source LLC
Chambersburg PA
CBHW041308110526
44590CB00028B/4289